D1741062

This book is for people in pursuit of perfect, luscious lips.

A journey dedicated to revealing the unique qualities

and hidden meaning behind everyone's smile.

Through love and understanding we can make a difference

with just one kiss.

A LITTLE BOOK ABOUT LIPS

First published in 2017 by Able Printing
www.ableprinting.com.au
Australia
Edited by Bev Ryan Publishing
www.bevryanpublish.com
Illustrated by Jim Frisino
www.gocaricatures.com
Cover & Design by Loma Larkings
www.ableprinting.com.au

Copyright © Janine Hall 2017
www.organiclipbalm.com.au

All rights reserved. Except as permitted under the Australian Copyright Act 1968, no part of this publication may be reproduced, stored in a retrieval system, or transmitted in any form or by any means, electronic, mechanical, photocopying, recording or otherwise, without the prior written permission from the publisher. All enquiries should be made to the author.

Title: One Million Kisses
Author: Janine Hall

ISBN: 978-0-6481390-0-3

Subject: Lip Care

DISCLAIMER
The material in this publication is of the nature of general comment only, and does not represent professional advice. It is not intended to provide specific guidance for particular circumstances and it should not be relied on as the basis of any decision to take action or not take action on any matter which it covers. Readers should obtain professional advice where appropriate, before making any such decision. To the maximum extent permitted by law, the author and publisher disclaim all responsibility and liability to any person, arising directly or indirectly from any person taking or not taking action based on the information in this publication.

One
Million Kisses

A little book about lips
and the secrets they reveal.

To my community, extended family and friends.

I would like to express my humble gratitude to you for without your support, our crazy conversations, hugs, laughter and everything in between you've helped me more than you will ever know. I am truly honored to have you in my world.

When your message becomes greater
than your fear
you have no choice but to step up
and share it

Kisses

Janine

To my family Colin, Tegan, Ryan and Jack
I love you x

About Janine

Janine is a wife and mother of three adult children living on the Sunshine Coast, Australia. Her holistic career began the day she saw an advertisement in the local paper for a remedial massage course, back in 2000.

Embracing study with three small children under the age of nine her new adventure was never going to be easy. Looking back, this was one of those profound moments in time. The voice inside her saying "Just do it!" became her driving force and the more she learnt about holistic living, the more she felt like she was coming home to her own body. Things just felt right.

In 2001 Janine was diagnosed with chemical poisoning and while undergoing professional treatment Janine became highly attuned to the healing benefits on a physical, spiritual, environmental and mental level or as she refers to it 'Holistic'. This knowledge was something Janine knew she must share with the world.

Her business started as a mobile massage clinic with a successful home based salon before opening a highly sort after Organic Day Spa which included her love of natural foods at the café she also owned.

Today, Janine has treated over 16,000+ clients for holistic skin and body care therapies. Drawing on her unique body intuitive intelligence, Janine has also developed a range of professional hand crafted skin care products including the world famous Organic Lip Balm.

Janine is the marketing and branding genius behind the rapid growth of The Organic Lip Balm Company's success story. In her first year she was awarded finalist for product sustainability in business and launched into the international arena.

Affectionately known as the lip lady to the stars, after her lip balms were gifted to Hollywood A-lists Top 40 Nominees celebrating Oscars weekend since 2016. Janine is Australia's leading expert in her field and believes that helping people just like you to be passionate about themselves is the key to being confident in your own smile!

Throughout all of her crazy adventures there has been one product that she has carried everywhere with her. A little lip balm she describes as a miracle balm, because it can literally fix almost anything.

The range is available online and shipped all over the world.

Janine has also leant her time to charities and cause related projects that inspire women to be happy and confident.

One Million Kisses

Introduction: What's so great about your lips?
Where it all began....
Science & history and body language

SECTION ONE:
Lip Health

SECTION TWO:
Understanding Lip Personalities

SECTION THREE:
Lip Print Readings

SECTION FOUR:
The Language of your Lips

SECTION FIVE:
Lip Care and Treatments

SECTION SIX:
One Kiss More

What's so great about your lips?

Have you ever wondered why we love our lips so much and yet neglect them at the same time? We use our lips to express so much of our personality, mostly subconsciously. We kiss, smile, laugh, talk, sing, shiver, touch, taste and feel with our lips. But how often do we really think about them?

You may be unaware that your lips are vitally important to your overall wellbeing and how you feel about yourself. With this thought in mind, this book is designed to take a closer look into the microsystem of our lips. It is meant to encourage you to think differently about your own pretty perfect smile, about what your lips reveal about you and how other people's lips can show their personality quirks.

Your body talks to you every day and your lips bring some very secret and often hidden truths to the mix. My goal is for you, while reading this book, to be able to laugh, share and indulge yourself and your girlfriends with a greater understanding of YOU! And them!

And of course I haven't left anything out, with some fun and fantastic tips, tricks and insights into some pretty handy health and beauty remedies, with a worldwide treasure trove of everything to do with lips, including injections, fillers and everything in between.

**I guarantee you will never look at your lips
in the same way ever again.**

You'll commonly hear lips described as: fat, skinny, thin, thick, voluminous, little, big, pouty, plump, fabulous, fake, gorgeous, hot, kissable, lush, lusty, full-bodied, curvy, classy, divine, dreamy, alluring, appealing, inflated, natural, nude, petite, pumped, pursed, rosebuds, rosy, sexy, swollen, tempting, voluptuous, wide, wet, hot, youthful, puffed, pretty, luscious, or large and that's just to name a few of the words used for lips.

My big, big epiphany came to me in late 2015. I had received some media interest in one of my products, my little lip balm that I have carried everywhere with me over the last 16 years. Following the publicity in the media, I received so many phone calls from complete strangers telling me their lip problems that I knew I had to share my knowledge and not keep it hidden any longer.

Hence this book, but I guess for me, the biggest realisation that I had to share what I knew really came when I opened my little market stall at the World Famous Eumundi Markets. I have many stories to share in this book but for now I will tell you about two women. One really a girl, of only around 12 and the other in her mid to late forties.

As people walk by my stall, I often get many stares and strange looks and what I like to call the market look of "bewilderment". I have some pretty amazing and eye-catching facts written up around the stall which most people have never heard before. It always seems to catch them by surprise and I often see people covering their lips as they read. I find this very amusing.

One day there was a young girl of around twelve walking by and she said at the top of her voice, "I have hideous lips", without even a second thought about what she had actually said, as if she was used to making these comments about herself.

And with that she was gone into the crowd.

I wanted to run up to her and teach her some cool and fun facts about her lips. But she was gone. Her words pulled at my heart - I could hear them ringing in my own ears hours after she had left. It was something I simply couldn't shake.

The other woman was in her mid forties. A dog had bitten her and torn her lips when she was only about eight years old.

She had endured months of surgery and skingraphs that had left a wide scar across her lips. At school she had been bullied and called names like "butt face" and other more hurtful names.

These names had left her heart broken, traumatised and self conscious about her appearance. She couldn't see what I saw, someone who was brave, a survivor and a kind, generous and beautiful woman with an infectious smile.

A LITTLE BOOK ABOUT LIPS

These are just two of the people who made me realise I had to write this little book on lips. My goal is to encourage you to think differently. To be mindful, and most importantly to laugh and love who you are.

I remember one day three gorgeous girls came to me and we started having a conversation about lips. Each woman had a different lip style, and the one with the thin top lip shared her desire to have injectables so that she could have that full voluminous lip look.

I started sharing with her all the qualities of her thin top lip, and asked her if she liked these traits. She was very impressed. Now I'm not sure if she changed her mind but I know I got her thinking about all the good things she had to offer, and that her lips were about more than simply being thin or full.

It is my goal, through sharing my knowledge and stories about lips, to inspire you to think differently and to treat yourself with kindness. Always to consider yourself as being of 'oneness'.

SECTION ONE Lip health

Chapter 1

Facts about your lips

I'm guessing that, like most people, you have never heard about your lip personality or that your lips' microsystem is related to the stomach and other organs.

Here's a thought: your lips define your entire personality, from how you handle conflict to how you love and live your life. It's a pretty cool way to think.

Your lips are your most expressive body feature after your eyes, and have more nerve endings than your genital area. On average, lips have 10,000 nerve endings whereas the female genitalia has approximately 8000 and the male genital area around 6000.

Lips are one of only 4 body parts that don't have any sebaceous glands, and are only 0.3 mm thick. If you pull apart a 2-ply tissue this gives you a good idea of how thick your lips actually are.

I've been fascinated with lips for a very long time, ever since I realised I could tell if someone was happy, angry or sad by their lips. I've also been able to use people's lips to help in recognising certain problems within the body.

I call this body reading.

I am a massage, beauty & intuitive healing therapist. I began, almost unconsciously, to recognise and diagnose internal and emotional issues in my clients. These clients were incredibly grateful for my treatment and my advice on practical solutions to fix their problems. Some clients have told me their sessions with me were life changing.

However, most people really don't think too much about their lips except for the often-heard words that they're unhappy with their lips' shape, lines, thickness or colour. We love applying lip colours and glosses and anything that enhances our own natural lips. But apart from that you probably have no idea of your lips' intricate and detailed microsystem.

Your lip area has been used as a diagnostic health check for over 3000 years. Long before MRIs, traditional Chinese medicine practitioners would use the lip ecosystem for their patients' health checks. They knew that each part of your body is linked to certain organs and emotional functions.

Here are eight health facts about your lips

1. Lips have no sebaceous glands;
2. Your top lip is linked to your stomach, spleen, and pancreas;
3. Your bottom lip is linked to your intestines;
4. Pale lips are indicators of a weak pancreas;
5. Cracked lips relate to digestive and stomach imbalances;
6. Sore lips are clues to allergies;
7. Soft pink lips are a sign you're in good health;
8. Your lips are the most sensitive part of your entire body.

Imagine for a moment that you continually have cracked lips and no matter what you do they stay the same. What if your solution to eliminating the cracked lips is to change the way you eat or to eliminate something from your diet?

When clients come to visit me, one of the biggest tell-tale signs of a food allergy is the lack of a clear pale pink outline to the lip area. It often can look almost smudged.

This book teaches you how to recognise health and emotional issues and can give you a better understanding of how to interact with someone. You may even find it helpful when hiring staff or wishing to work with other people.

When it comes to beauty products and procedures, the industry has seen nothing like the rise of the phenomenon of injectables since the 1940s, when red lipstick became the must-have fashion accessory. And the redder the better!

Since 2002 there has been an entire industry built around women not liking their lips. In fact, in 2015 in the USA alone an injectable lip treatment was performed every 19 minutes. The industry has grown over **800%**.

In Australia nearly 2 million injectables were performed in 2015 and this rapid increase has shown no sign of slowing down, because women have been brain-washed into wanting more voluptuous-looking lips - because they are under the impression that having lips that look fuller will make them appear more confident, sexy, happy and likeable.

My goal is that by the end of this book you will be looking at your lips in a whole different light and be wanting to take care of them a little better. You'll learn to uncover more about your internal, emotional and physical well being. I want you to be able to say; "Hey I like my lips because..." and to have a whole lot fun doing the exercises and following along with the many tips and tricks throughout this book.

*So pucker up
and let's get your pout on!*

Lips are only
0.3mm thick
and the
most sensitive
part
of the body

Chapter 2

Lip anatomy

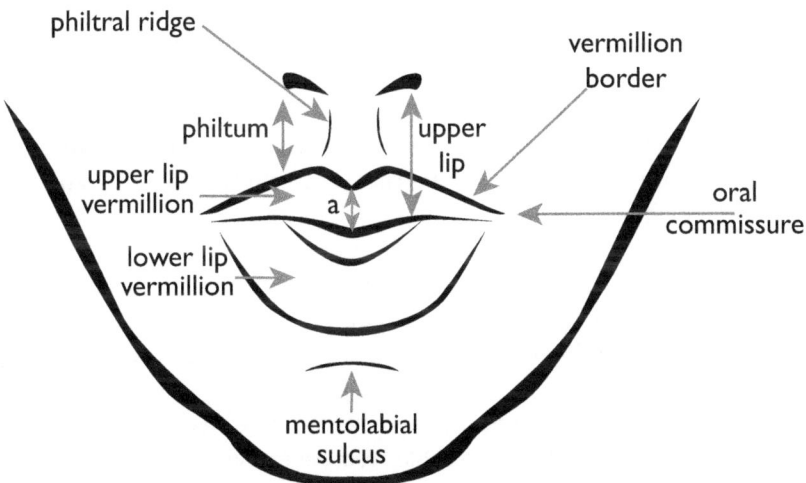

Your lips are defined by pink melanocytes around the top and bottom of your mouth. Your lip area actually starts from the base of your nose, the section called the philtrum. This area alone can reveal how stubborn you may be or if you are more adventurous. *I will teach you about the philtrum and what it means in Section 3, Chapter 7.*

The upper lip vermillion is the pink space on the upper lip that stops at the side of the mouth, which is known as the oral commissure. The oral commissure enables the mouth to open and close. The lower lip vermillion is the pink space of the lower lip.

The vermillion on both top and bottom lips is recognised as the epidermis (skin) that is externally highly keratinized (pink) and internally keratinized (white). This indicates the difference between the cellular growth. This also happens with nails and hair. The upper and lower lips where the skin turns pink have no sebaceous glands.

Lips come in different shapes and sizes which reflect an individual's personality and life path and challenges.

Your upper lip also represents your **heart centre**, commonly referred to as the *cupids bow*. Although this is not an anatomical term it is most definitely a personality term which helps define the different depths and insider secrets of your personality.

The bottom of the lip is also defined by an arch on the bottom lip directly underneath the heart centre.

Lips also represent certain metaphysical energy systems. Your **heart chakra** is found directly in the centre of the *cupids bow* on the upper lip and runs straight through to the bottom lip.

The upper lip is how you see yourself in the world and focuses on the physical and emotional feelings that you bring to your life. And the lower lip is how the world sees you and what you have come to do on your soul's journey.

There is quite a distinction between the two, as what you do, have and experience in this world and what you have come to experience, create and learn can often be entirely different. This has a lot to do with what you feel is right and what you think the world wants to see.

When you break down your lip anatomy and the different sections and what they mean, you will see them as much more than something to kiss, colour, smile, eat or have conversations with.

Every part of your lips tells and shares a story. Imagine for a moment that you are about to meet someone who is really important to you, or perhaps you are on a blind date and you want to understand a little bit more about this person.

You would like the person to be open to what you have to say, yet for some reason you find that the conversation is going nowhere. Your companion is mostly unresponsive and sits with closed mouth or barely smiles. This would be a key indicator that the person either isn't interested in what you have to say or may not be a willing participant in your date.

Does the person bite his/her lip when looking at you? Is his/her mouth red and sore? Perhaps the lips are pursed and tight, which could indicate that the person may have something to hide and is not being entirely honest.

You owe it to yourself to discover more about this person and learning how to understand lips could be the easiest way to uncovering new relationships.

There are 7 key elements to understanding a person's lip language: width, shape, size, colour, depth, lines, health

1. **Width:** do the lips end inside or outside the direct line of the eye pupil's iris?
2. **Shape:** are they round and pouty or flat?
3. **Size:** are they thin or thick or just right?
4. **Colour:** are they pale pink or red or something in between?
5. **Depth (protrusion):** does the top lip protrude over the bottom lip, or vice versa?
6. **Lines:** are their lines above, along, or within the lips, or are they smooth and flat?
7. **Health:** are there cold sores, cancerous cells, black spots, or millia?

Learning how to recognise and understand these key elements are easy when you know what you're looking for.

In Section 2, Chapter 4, I'll go into more detail on the 7 key elements and you will gain a better understanding of both the key elements' physical and metaphysical (emotional) meaning.

Have you ever wondered why there is so much emphasis on having fuller bigger lips? People feel really insecure around their lips, especially if they're thin or full of lines.

Have you ever thought that altering your lips with fillers, injections and implants could be destroying your life path?

There are certainly bigger reasons behind this, which you're about to learn. You see, the fuller the lips are, the more confident, fun and happy a person is perceived as being, while lips of a thinner nature may leave you feeling inadequate and less confident.

This book teaches through practical and personal life stories, giving you a better understanding of what your lips reveal about your health and well being. This book will teach you how you can improve every relationship you have and especially the one with yourself.

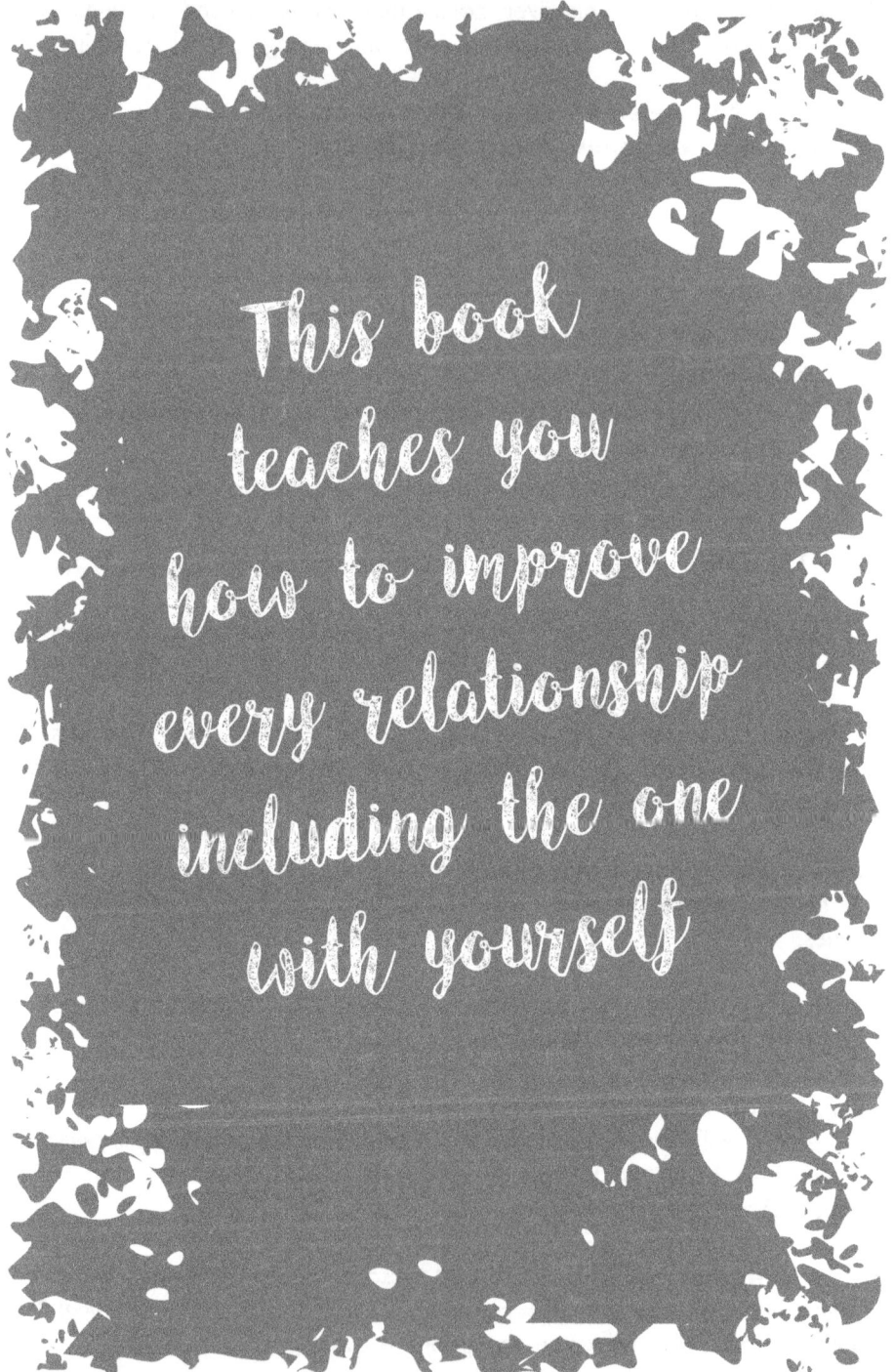

This book
teaches you
how to improve
every relationship
including the one
with yourself

Chapter 3

Understanding your body

1. Your lips don't have sebaceous glands

Lip anatomy: Sebaceous glands excrete an oil called sebum which helps keep your skin moist and protects it from environmental elements such as wind, sun etc. Lips are one of 4 body parts that don't contain sebaceous glands.

Lip emotion / metaphysical: Self-confidence means an ability to let go of whatever no longer serves you. It means holding yourself in good value and self worth. Enlarged and clogged pores may be indicators that you lack confidence and are devaluing yourself. *Common thoughts: "I'm not good enough or I can't do that".*

Key indicators of imbalances: Cold sores, pimples, cracks and redness.

2. Your top lip is linked to your stomach

Lip anatomy: Everything starts in the stomach and this plays a major role in your entire health. It breaks down food, turns it into liquid and then passes it through the intestinal tract.

Lip emotion / metaphysical: Emotional things are becoming indigestible to you. You can't stomach certain things about your life or certain situations of your past. You see yourself as a victim or powerless to change. Unwilling to let go.

Key indicators of imbalances: Red outline of the vermillion, smudged appearance of top lip, food allergies, pimples and cancer sores.

A LITTLE BOOK ABOUT LIPS

3. Your bottom lip is linked to your intestines

Lip anatomy: Your intestines helps pass out solid waste through the rectum and assist with the elimination of whatever no longer serves us both on a physical and metaphysical. May start to develop self image and become a perfectionist to one's self. May also judge others very harshly.

Lip emotion / metaphysical: Emotions of grief, sadness and loss. Suffering from lung conditions could mean you can become irritable and irrational at times.

Key indicators of imbalances: Deep lines and cracks on bottom lip, diarrhea, constipation, lethargy.

4. Cracked lips relate to digestive issues

Lip anatomy: Indicates dehydration, eating hard to digest foods such as dairy and wheat products.

Lip emotion / metaphysical: Unable to stomach things in your life, resulting in feelings of being stuck and unappreciated.

Key indicators of imbalances: Red, cracked and peeling lips, often a large crack in the centre of your bottom lip.

5. Pale lips are indicators of a weak pancreas

Lip anatomy: The pancreas supports the stomach in the digestion of food. A weak pancreas could mean that you have a slow sluggish metabolism and suffer from being lethargic.

Lip emotion / metaphysical: Feelings of being boxed in or unable or unwilling to see change as being good, not wishing to change. Assists in feelings of happiness and/or sadness if feeling stressed and able to cope. Being intelligent and brain function.

Key indicators of imbalances: Sugar cravings, and cold sores on the upper right hand side, headaches and licking of lips, sleepy and or unable to sleep, constipation.

6. Soft pink lips mean you're in good health

Lip anatomy: This is what we should all be wanting - beautiful pink coloured lips with no spots, brown marks or lesions on them.

Lip emotion / metaphysical: Indicates you're in good health and your internal body is copy and working well. Able to cope with ease and are not resistant to change.

Key indicators of balances: Smiling, good colour to lip, defined vermillion, no excessive lines or cracks.

7. Sore lips are a clue to allergies

Lip anatomy: Can indicate problems in the reproductive system and eating the wrong foods. Can be allergic to lip care ingredients.

Lip emotion / metaphysical: If your lips are often bright red, you could be suffering from high blood pressure. Feelings of being unsupported, more often on an emotional level rather than physical.

Key indicators of imbalances: Undefined vermillion or red line around outside of mouth, dry and continually licking.

Soft
pink lips
mean you're
in
good health

Chapter 4

Lip
health warnings

1. Upturned lines: On the corner of the mouth can indicate stomach disorders.

2. Cracks in the corners: Lacking good nutrients and vitamins; dehydrated.

3. White lines: Can indicate that you are anemic, and often suffering from irregular bowel movements.

4. Purple lines: Breathing issues and blood disorders. High blood pressure.

5. Mottled appearance: Weak liver, lungs, pancreas and spleen.

6. Many upper fine lines: Reproductive issues, with problems in conception and ovulation, and period pains. Males may suffer from irregular and/or awkward sperm.

7. Crisscross lines and diagonal lines: Hormonal imbalances, mood swings, and possible bouts of depression.

8. Loose large lips: Are a sign of uncontrollable physical and emotional feelings. Over inflated egos compared to the actual reality. Emotionally self-centred whilst serving others.

9. Tight lips: Internal anger, the need to control situations that are uncontrollable (meaning not originating from you). Sex may be painful at times. Lips are even and look compressed inwards. Often negative feelings of emotionless behavior. May be unrealistically demanding.

10. Cold sores: Anger about one's self. Always putting yourself down. " I can't, I'm not good enough, I'm not normal". Feelings of discontent about where life is heading.

11. Cancerous cells: Internal anger, feeling of being misunderstood and not speaking up. Food allergies, or too much substance abuse.

12. Millia around lips: Weak pancreas; too much sugar, fat and meat. Body is clogged and may suffer from constipation or diarrhea. Headaches could be common.

13. Black/brown Spots: Liver disease or weak liver. Unable to see beyond hurts. Suppressed anger. Poor diet and eating the wrong foods. Body unable to digest and doesn't recognise what you are feeding it.

14. Red lips: Poor diet, digestive system not coping with your choices. Eat easily digestible foods. Avoid processed foods, dairy, wheat, sugars, alcohol, medications.

Chapter 1

The eleven different personality styles

Lip No 1: Alluring

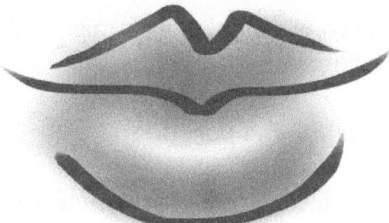

Lip Type: Prominent arched/peak in heart centre in arch, upturned lip corner, smaller lip width. Fuller bottom lip and slightly thinner top lip

Celebrity lips: Taylor Swift

Characteristics: You can be described as funny, witty and adorable and people simply love your wit. You have a majestic feeling that radiates around you. Hence your large circle of friends. You have many loves throughout your life. But there will be one that will simply be everything to you.

Strengths: You dedicate yourself to your cause, and are a great animal lover. You're a fantastic listener and can read between the lines of what's 'NOT' being said to give you greater insight into any situation.

Your voice is very powerful in a courageous way and when you speak people listen with intent and want to help you in anyway they can.

Vulnerability: You wear your heart on your sleeve and are deeply passionate. You fear being alone and don't stay single for long. You don't like to sit still for too long as you may have a bout of **FOMO** (fear of missing out). You may at times be unwittingly seducing the wrong person.

Lip No 2: Lavish

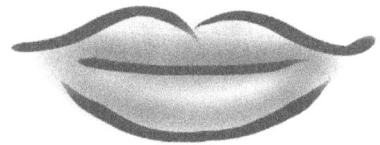

Lip Type: Thinner lips on top, wide lips, often straighter / rounded heart centre, bottom lip slightly protruding.

Celebrity lips: Elizabeth Taylor, Eva Longoria

Characteristics: You love the finer things in life, which is good as they naturally come to you. You expect and receive nothing but excellence. You're an incredibly generous person who gives as much as you receive, in love and kindness. You're a passionate lover.

Strengths: Your passion and perfectionism works well to attract everything that you desire. You love giving to charities and organising worthy events that you are enthusiactic about.

Vulnerability: You're a perfectionist, which makes you at times difficult to live with as you don't understand how people can be so blasé and laid-back about some things.

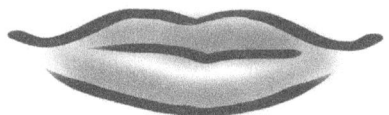

Lip Type: Lip thinned on top and bottom, wider lipped smile, rounded to flat heart centre. Slightly uneven lips or smile.

Celebrity: Princess Katherine

Characteristics: Softly spoken and incredibly loyal. Once you are someone's friend you are there for life.

Your busy and often hectic schedule means that you may not see your friends often. However, they know you're only a phone call away. You're a great problem solver and fix almost any situation with your rational thinking. You prefer classical music to heavy metal/rock. Ed Sheeran style to AC-DC.

You will make time for your inner circle of friends and family, to whom you are devoted and loyal, as they are to you. Your kindness and generosity is impeccable and you have many environmental and social causes that you are passionate about.

Strengths: Your loyalty to others often sees you in important roles that carry a lot of trust.

Vulnerability: You can sometimes take things too personally and feel that when something negative is said it is a personal attack on you. You often appear serious but you are merely deep in thought.

Lip No 4: Timeless

Lip Type: Wide lip, slightly fuller bottom lip, upturned corner, thinner top lip, almost equal top and bottom lips, rounded and flatter heart centre

Celebrity: Reese Witherspoon

Characteristics: If you heard people talking about you, they would say, "you look good for your age". You are healthy, and don't let things get you down too much. You're a great multi tasker and manage events and people with ease. You're highly creative and ideas easily flow through. You sometimes don't know how you will ever get through all of your plans.

Strengths: You are passionate, calming and energising. If someone wants something done, they ask you. No matter how full your schedule is you'll do it with ease and grace (seemingly). Well organised, sometimes through the chaos.

Vulnerability: You don't like to sit still. And because of this you find it very difficult to just be and can feel lost if there is not a project on the go, big or small it doesn't matter to you. You tend to find that you could personally feel a little guilty when it comes to family and spending time with them. You need to schedule in down time as much as your creative time. Make this a priority in your life and everything flows.

Lip No 5: Classic

Lip Type: Full top lip yet slightly up turned almost symmetrical with bottom lips, with upturned yet smaller arch on bottom with rounded heart centre. Wide lip.

Celebrity: Charlize Theron, Megan Fox, Natalie Portman

Characteristics: You like the simple things in life and aren't too bothered by bright shiny new objects. You don't go for the latest trends; instead you find your own style and stick to it. You love looking for the perfect things in out-of-the-way places. What others might see as junk, you see as lost treasure and can turn anything you find into your own creation. You prefer gardens, beaches and parks to high rises and buildings. You love riding a push bike whenever you can. Fresh air instead of air conditioning.

Strengths: You have a noble attitude to life which sees you make many choices carefully. You're not a procrastinator, but you won't make decisions in haste. You prefer to know what you want before you get it.

Vulnerability: You don't like causing a scene or upsetting anyone. If there is a discussion to be had, you'll be the one trying to make things right. You sometimes get angry when you feel you're not being heard.

Lip Type: Definite arched heart centre, full top and bottom lips almost even. Smaller width lips.

Celebrity: Rihanna

Characteristics: Funny, witty and undeniably attractive, which you subconsciously use to your advantage, often unaware of your own charm. People very rarely say no to you, simply because you are charismatic. You have many high and lows and aren't afraid to share them. At times you could be referred to as a diva. If you don't get your own way, you could be a little moody but people love you anyway.

Strengths: You're as strong & powerful as you are gentle, kind and generous. There's never a dull moment when you're around. You are thinking creatively all the time and are as open about your faults and flaws as you are about how fabulous you are, which is an adoring quality that people love about you.

Vulnerability: You can be an emotional rollercoaster, experiencing any number of moods within a short period of time. Anything from happy and cheerful, to moody and sulky. You may suffer from depression.

Lip Type: Smaller width lips but with a wide smile, high curved/rounded heart centre. Thinner top lip, fuller bottom lip.

Celebrity: Madonna

Characteristics: You're powerful and well educated. And you know exactly what to do in any situation. You've studied hard to be where you are, and can talk politics, babies, fashion and the stock market all in one sentence. You're the perfect hostess for any major event. "Fear and I can't" isn't in your vocabulary.

If you don't know something you learn. People are drawn to you for your wit and conversational skills. You can make your audience laugh as easily as making them cry. You love a good costume party and don't mind being the centre of attention.

Strengths: You have a very warm and kind heart that wants to give and be loved. You are very warm hearted and love giving and receiving hugs. People love your company and love being with you.

Vulnerability: You may find it difficult to keep a long-term relationship or attract a partner, as many believe that you don't need anyone else in your life. You appear to be self sufficient yet long for your equal to show up.

However, if you do attract your soul mate earlier in life you will have a strong foundation for a lifetime of love, often experiencing many different relationships with the one long-term partner.

Lip Type: Slightly rounded heart centre, thinner lip on top than bottom, wide mouth lip. Slightly upturned bottom lip.

Celebrity: Gwyneth Paltrow, Jennifer Aniston

Characteristics: You are determined to make things happen and to get it right. If at first you don't succeed you'll keep trying. You often don't walk away from things until you have exhausted every possible situation. You wear your heart on your sleeve and are very thoughtful. Most of the time you follow a healthy lifestyle but may have one or two vices that you simply love to indulge in.

Strengths: You are soft, funny, and enthusiastic. Incredibly ambitious and people naturally trust you. You want your natural skills, integrity and determination to speak for themselves. Preferring to use your brains as opposed to your beauty. You don't step on people's toes or would knowingly ever hurt people. You have the amazing ability to see the positive in any situation.

Vulnerability: Even though you are determined you do everything with integrity and trust other people to do the right thing. As a result you may sometimes find yourself being the victim of other people's untrustworthy actions. This, however, will never keep you down long because of the positive way you view the world.

Lip No 9: Elegant

Lip Type: Fuller upper and bottom lip, with top being slightly fuller. Narrow arched heart centre. Wide lip and upturned smile.

Celebrity: Julia Roberts, Angelina Jolie, Serena Williams

Characteristics: You are cultured, imaginative and dainty. Preferring the softer side of things, you love being in natural environments. You love a good laugh and can often laugh at yourself. But there is gentle tender side to you that simply surpasses everything that you do. Generous, kind and forthright. You can't help but tell the truth. People feel beautiful in your company as you naturally put them at ease. You don't sweat the small stuff.

Strengths: When you speak, you do this so eloquently that you draw a crowd and people want to know what you have to say. People are drawn to your kindness and value your opinion.

Vulnerability: Your honesty can often be hard to hear especially if someone has asked for opinion on something.

Lip Type: Full lip top and bottom with wide and big smile, slightly curved and rounded heart centre

Celebrity: Oprah, Michelle Obama

Characteristics: You are fearless, self assured and enterprising, which has not been without your own struggles. However, your natural ability to change the way things are done makes you shine. Commanding respect and often in a position of authority of the highest regard. You change the rules and people follow. If you've been told you can't do something you will make a point of doing it and doing it better than anyone else. This isn't because you like to show off or be a diva - in fact you're the opposite. You often do things yourself to show others how to do it. People are drawn to your enthusiasm and entrepreneurial skills. You have an incredibly generous side and enjoy the art of giving.

Strengths: You are the game changer and are seen as a trail blazer. What once seemed impossible is now truth. You are often highly paid at whatever you do.

Vulnerability: Your passion may be seen as feisty at times. But your diplomatic people skills will shine through.

Lip Type: Small thin width top and bottom, with often closed wide smile or smirk. More common in men.

Celebrity: Robbie Williams, Ronan Keating, David Beckham

Characteristics: You have chosen a life of solitude which suits you perfectly, even if your career is in the public eye. You love your own company and enjoy the stillness of life. You will more than likely avoid shopping centres and any crowded places. Because you love your own company you will often only have a small circle of near and dear friends and meeting new people at times could be difficult for you.

Strengths: You are also very determined and you have a tendency to be incredibly powerful when it comes to manifesting what you really want. You are driven and not afraid to show your softer side to someone special and to only a few of your inner circle. You are incredibly loyal to your friends.

Vulnerability: Being in relationships that make you feel boxed in can prove difficult. The person with whom you are in a relationship will need to understand this and give you space to relish in your own self.

You are the quiet fun one who doesn't tend to draw attention to yourself. However, your coping mechanism to cover your shyness is that you are more likely to develop an ultra-ego (persona) for public outings. You could be more susceptible to addictions.

It's time
to love
your lips

Chapter 2

Lip personality traits
(elementals)

Have you ever heard of archangels, fairies and other mythical creatures? They tend to be the heroes and villains in movies. Characters such as tinkerbell, unicorns, mermaids, dragons, werewolves, trolls, pegasus, leprechauns, gnomes, elves, nymphs and goblins.

You will also find mentions of Zeus, Isis, Medusa, Aphrodite, Athena, Archangel Michael and the Angel Gabriel, to name a few mythical characters.

Introducing the elementals side, or your lip personality traits, gives you an even greater understanding of who you are as a person, what career you will be drawn to, what type of friends you will have and how you are seen in society.

The elemental side of your lip personality:

Your lips have distinct characteristics of both your physical and metaphysical world.

Lip No 1. Alluring

Your earthly element is that of a mermaid and you love hanging out at the water. You often have longer hair and don't like wearing it short. In fact you have only ever experienced having short hair a few times in your life as it feels uncomfortable to you. You love to act on a whim and spread your joy wherever possible. You are grounded and keep calm on most occasions unless there are rough seas when you will likely swish your tail (or voice) to be heard. You have a tiny waist, long necks and slim arms. A mermaid loves to gather things, whether they are earthly elements or not, such as coins, shells, crystals, cards, books, pens, perfumes, oils. You will have your favourite collection that you simply live by.

A LITTLE BOOK ABOUT LIPS

Lip No 2. Lavish

Your earthly element is that of a deva in Dame or Knighthood. Kind and generous. Your body is most likely shorter and fuller although as a young deva you were quite skinny with a small waist. Over time your body changed with your deva ways. Medium to large breasts. You can be quite dramatic in getting your point across but rest assured, people pay attention to you. You strive for excellence and are quite worldly. You adorn yourself with jewels of diamonds and crystals, and feel naked without them. The jewels are part of your dress code and it would be very rare to see you wearing none. Even in the shower you are reluctant to take them off.

Lip No 3. Tender

Your earthly element is that of a fairy with dragonfly wings. You know exactly what you like and being true to yourself is one of the key compliments to your earthly body. You also don't take yourself too seriously (although sometimes you may appear to be) and can often see the brighter, funnier side of life. You are quite timid and fine in your stature although this is rather tall for a fairy.

Your dragonfly wings give you the ability to change hats and roles quite quickly and you are very adaptable to your surroundings. You have quite a slim build, with the long straight fingers that help to hold your magic wand. You have almond shaped eyes which match your lips and dragonfly wings. You don't have pouty or 'flirtatious' lips.

You're not bothered by extremely fancy things. Although it's lovely to have them you would also be happy in small cottage/home as long as you are with the people you love. You're most comfortable in nature.

Lip No 4: Timeless

Your earthly element is that of the nymphs who are well known for their seamless beauty. They are referred to as being playful and creative. You love to listen to people's problems and offer sound and helpful advice. As a nymph you are likely to be at home amongst the trees, mountains, rivers and streams. You are strong in stature but are neither too slim or too buxom. A feeling of just right is what suits you best. You seem to have the perfect height to weight ratio and although you know you are appealing to the opposite sex you neither play up or down your feelings or emotions, preferring to use your brains and wit to get your point across. You are very helpful, generous and a great problem solver. You are neither too tall or short.

Lip No 5. The Classic

Your earthly element is that of a pixie. You like everything to be just right and you'll fly around fixing things up until they are neat and tidy. You don't like clutter and love being at home. Your happy place is around a table with friends or family, laughing and being silly. You don't mind cooking scrummy meals.

You like to joosh things up and love being and playing the decorating pixie. Including transforming and makeovers for your friends. You can wear your hair any way. However you are most comfortable with it shorter than shoulder length and you love wearing it as short as a 'pixie cut'. You have a finer skeletal system with slightly longer arms, tiny waist, and you are generally just over 5ft to medium height.

Lip No 6. Pampered

Your earthly element is that of the Goddess Ishtar who struggles with boundaries. You love to help others, sometimes too much, and wonder why things sometimes back fire. You're always willing to give someone a second and third chance as you honestly believe in them. However, this can often be to your own detriment and it can appear to backfire, especially when you want more than the person receiving does. You may at times feel zapped of energy, which leaves you feeling depleted. This is your lesson to learn throughout your life of the balance of giving and receiving. Your bodily elements are that of slightly smaller to 5ft 6". You may have a voluptuous derriere that mimics your lips.

Lip No 7. Divine Goddess

Your earthly element is that of the Goddess Isis. You are strong, capable and fierce when you need to be. You are often tall with broader shoulders and a slightly broader waist, although still in proportion. You are the teacher to women on how to live the life you desire. You can act as a medicine woman with your cures for all, including relationships. You can lead as well as you follow and often start your role as a follower before jumping the reins as the leader. You do this to be amongst the 'people' to gain more respect, as you see yourself no different to them. You want to walk their walk and then show them how to lead by doing it yourself. You see yourself as merely a teacher who is capable of speaking up. You are often taller in stature and stand no less that 5ft 6".

Lip No 8. Sweetheart

Your earthly element is that of the Goddess Macha (Mock-uh) who shares a love of the land with other goddesses. She likes to make right what is wrong and stands for what she believes in. Quite gentle and fierce when she needs to be. Your wit is your best power and you can soon determine right from wrong. You don't like to be fooled or made a fool of but you do have an incredible sense of humour. You'll often wear the colour red or have red in your home. You like things to be fair and just. However, if they're not you're a good person to have on the team to right any wrongs. You are blessed with the ability to love more than once in your life. Each one more special than the last. It's through your learnings of love that you find your strength. You are often built quite lean and tall (5ft 7" - 8") and can be good at running and sports. You love the simplicity of life.

Lip No 9. Elegant

Your earthly element is that of the Goddess Mawu, who is gentle and kind. She loves teaching about the earth's elements. You will find you love being in the garden and can be quite the vegetable grower (or herbs). You love the connection to soil and earth and have a high regard for people who can see the beauty from nothing. You can appear to be a loner although you do enjoy the company of others. You're graceful in your approach to almost everything you do, and have the patience of a saint; nothing appears to be too much trouble or hassle for you as you simply go about your business one task at a time. You are of solid build often having equal hip and shoulder length apart.

Lip No 10 Courageous

Your earthly element is that of the Goddess Aphrodite, the saviour to all and an eternal soul who sees the good in everything she does. She is a warrior of love, beauty and kindness despite what myths says. Love is her highest calling and she genuinely wants to help you. Seeing beauty in everything you touch. Aphrodite has many gifts beyond the physical of simply being, which is why many people are naturally drawn to her. You are naturally attracted to all things in nature and find great peace sitting and admiring.

Lip No 11: Mystic

Your earthly element is that of Zeus, who is considered to be a leader and warrior amongst men. You are often put into positions of leadership and fame, despite your personal need for privacy. You have great strength, power and charisma and people are uncommonly drawn to you, which is why you can be considered incredibly reserved and almost shy at times.

You are a warrior for your family and will more than likely only have what you consider to be one family, despite many other opportunities for growing and sowing seeds of fertility.

Your lips
have distinct
characteristics
that represent
the physical
and metaphysical
worlds

Chapter 3

Lip Characteristics

Now that you understand and have a general idea about your overall personality, you might like to learn that each part of your lips has its own character, which tells more of your unique lip story.

A lip characteristic can be easily defined simply by looking at the shape of your own or someone else's lips.

Characteristic 1: Naturally full lips - tend to have strong motherly tendencies. Mother to others, including friends, lovers, children, community.

Characteristic 2: Wide lips - generous with their time, strong giver within the community.

Characteristic 3: Narrow lips - cautious with their time and like to have their own needs met before helping others.

Characteristic 4: Heart centre - (top middle lip) large and prominent, curved like an M, can be powerful communicators. People listen to what they say but they need to be careful.

Characteristic 5: Lower arch - (bottom middle lip) kind and make great carers of others as they often put others' needs first before their own.

Characteristic 6: Top lip - their feminine side and how they see themselves in the world.

Characteristic 7: Bottom lip - the masculine side and how the world sees them.

Characteristic 8: Full bottom lip - strong and stable, will often be leaders in their field .

Characteristic 9: Thin bottom lip - dependable in a supportive way and like to keep in the back ground. A perfect personal assistant to high profile people. Like to have people around them and can feel lonely often.

Characteristic 10: Straight top lip - may often have trouble with boundaries in relationships. Pretty even in temperament and don't like a lot of drama.

Chapter 4

The seven key lip elements

When it comes to beginning to understand lip personalities there are 7 key elements that really help you learn and match the characteristics of each person's individual lip.

1. Width: Do the lips end inside or outside the direct line of the eyes' pupils?

Lip width is defined by where the corner of your mouth ends. A wide mouth is defined as ending outside the black pupil area when you look straight ahead. A small width mouth is defined by finishing inside your pupil area when you look straight ahead.

2. Shape: Are they round and pouty or flat?

Would you best describe your lips as round pouty or flat? It's best to turn sideways and see how your lips look. Round and pouty lips will have a definite curve of the vermillion area. Whereas flat lips will be almost in a straight line with no sideways curve.

3. Size: Are they thin or thick or just right?

Would you describe your lips as thin or thick or perhaps a bit of both? Most people will have varying degrees of either thickness or thinness of their lips. Both the top and bottom will vary with one being thinner whilst the other is thicker.

4. Colour: Pale pink or red or something in between?

Are your lips a consistent pale pink or are they often red?

5. Depth (protrusion): Do they protrude top or bottom over or under the lips.

The depth or protrusion refers to the middle of either your upper or lower lips and is defined as the section in the middle of either. Sometimes you can have an uneven lip area with a protrusion towards the side of your vermillion area.

6. Lines: Are there lines above, along, or within your lips, or are they smooth and flat?

Lines are defined as either on the top lip and just above and in the area of the philtrum as well as lines on your lips and lower lip lines. Lines are also prevalent at the corners of your mouth.

7. Health: Are there cold sores, cancerous cells, black spots, or millia?

Do you have cold sores, millia (small white pimple like hard lumps), black spots and different shades of pink or red? Are these marks on the bottom or top of the lip? Or in the corner of the mouth?

Chapter 5
Most valuable lip expressions

You may not be aware but your lips give away how you're feeling even on a subconscious level.
Here are four of the most famous lip expressions and their meanings.

1. Pout: A pursed pout is a good indication that you are not quite sure of a situation or you are feeling a little bit cheeky. A pout can also indicate that you don't believe what someone is telling you.

By pursing you are keeping your true feelings hidden and unspoken. Why is pouting a common look when it comes to selfies? It's because it is believed to be more alluring and sexy and give just a hint of shyness.

2. Large smile: There are three main reasons why you want to give a large smile to someone. Either you want to impress or you want that someone to like you. And the other reason is you are very familiar with the person you are smiling at and like, know and trust them.

3. Small / closed mouth smile: Can indicate that your not quite sure of what someone could be saying to you. You also want to keep something to yourself. And perhaps even though you may not know them, you still want to feel approachable and liked by this someone. An example of this is when you walk by someone on a morning walk; you will often either say hello or use a small closed mouth smile.

4. Licking / biting: There can be a few very good reasons why you might be licking your lips: one is to get something off them - perhaps you have a little too much chocolate ganache or you've accidently left a line of milk from your morning coffee and not been made aware of it, until one of your friends kindly starts doing weird things to get you to wipe your face.

On the other hand, if someone begins to lick and bite their lips when meeting you it could be a really good indicator that they may find you attractive, especially if they are licking their bottom lip.

It could also mean that they feel like they are in trouble and may have something to hide.

A LITTLE BOOK ABOUT LIPS

Getting your lip body language correct
and learning to read your lips
or someone else's
can become a great icebreaker.

Section Three Lip Print readings

Chapter 1

Understanding lip prints

What is the purpose of lip reading?

A lip reading is an ancient technique used to diagnose certain healthy conditions; it is as much a science as it is intuitive. Learning how to understand each aspect of your lip print is a great way to learn more about yourself and a truly remarkable way of having a healing.

Your lip print describes your life's journey, what you have come here to accomplish and many other unique things about yourself. Unlike a palm reading, your lip print can change from hour to hour depending on what is on your mind at the time and what you are processing. It truly is that amazing.

This healing and body reading modality has been a lost art form but was used by traditional Chinese medicine practitioners and traditional healers, body language experts and psychics.

Facial reading has been an interpretive way of systematically recognising health concerns and emotional behaviour for over 3000 years.

Your **LIPS** story begins by taking a closer look at your lip characteristics, personality and print. Followed by your lips elemental guides, physical health, relationships, careers, and your quirky personality traits.

These findings can determine your likes, dislikes, vulnerabilities, natural characteristics and any health concerns. This can really help you understand why you may do things or react in a certain way.

During your **L-I-P-S** you will learn more about your vulnerabilities, characteristics and strengths, which is a great *life* tool to keep handy when it comes to making choices. Your lips are closely related to the **chakra** system, which reveals much about your emotional well being and energy centres.

When you combine your personalised lip print with your other characteristics you begin to get a much better understanding of yourself — what your likes and dislikes are and how you are as a person. This often leads to being more tolerant of others when you understand their own personalised traits and why they do things, and most importantly why they are different to you.

Your lip print is a microsystem within the art of facial reading.

Chapter 2

How to give your self a lip print reading

You will need
- dark red lipstick,
- a piece of paper,
- if you have one a magnifying glass,
- and don't forget your sense of humour.

The four steps on how to give yourself a lip print reading.

1. Your first step is to apply your lipstick.

2. Next smooch the paper like you would if you were kissing some one. Simply place your hands/fingers behind the paper and press your lips on the paper, close to its left side.

3. Take a deep breath to clear and calm your thoughts and smooch it again, in the centre.

4. Another deep breath and smooch it a third time, on the right, so that you have three lips smooches across the page from left to right. This is similar to a three intuitive card drawing/reading.

These three prints represent your past, present and future. I suggest giving yourself a regular reading, perhaps every season to keep you on the right track.

We will now look at the shape, colour, width and lines of your prints.

Your
lips print
is a microsystem
within
the art of
facial reading

Chapter 3

What your lip shapes reveal

Four shapes:

There are four common shapes that best describe how you physically like to do things and how you like to experience your life. These are the characteristics that help you stay focused and organised in your daily life.

Look at your lip print and see which shape best describes yours.

Round: It has no defined corners and has quite an open circle feeling to it. This type of lip print means that you are more likely to go with the flow of things, and you tend not to be too distracted by detail. You are often creative and you won't like paper work too much. Having an office job would become boring for you. You are very even-tempered and have the ability to fit in anywhere. You are easy to get along with in most cases. You can be the leader or a great team player as long as you are passionate about what you are doing. You are 100% committed to everything that you do.

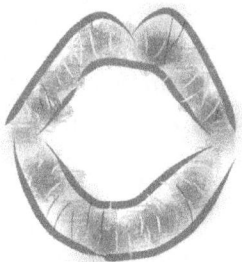

Abstract: Does your lip print tend to look like it has 5-7 edges and has no real clearly defined shape? If so then you have what I call the abstract print and you are a highly efficient and unique individual. Your life will have every ebb and flow possible in it. Some people may think that you are best described as a little aloof. However, what you really need to know is that this type of print indicates that you are more artistic than you are aware of. You like things to do with nature, outdoors and the arts.

You like not having any plans and love doing things on a whim. You love working in teams and creating projects while helping others. You are great with charities and humanitarian work.

Triangle: You can describe this type of print as a flat bottom and a pointy top lip and it truly does look like a triangle. Triangles are often very grounded people with a good strong and steady friendship base. You are best suited to jobs where you can climb to the top and which are challenging to you personally. You can also work very well as a key support person to help creative people bring their dreams to life. You are the doer and make things happen.

Rectangle: This print can be clearly defined by the sides and looks like a rectangular box. You are ordered and love a job that involves working with paper. You love order, routines and don't do too well with surprises, although you will organise one for someone else with pleasure. You do this because you love organising stuff in a structured and measured way. You are clean and tidy and hate things untidy; in fact if you work with abstract lip people you will drive each other around the bend.

You will know a lot of people in communities all over the globe and can make great connections with others and love the aspect of joining and connecting people and projects.

Chapter 4

Understanding lip widths

There are four main lip print widths that you need to consider:

1. Small - under 3 cm;
2. Large - 4.5 cm and above;
3. Thin - under 3 cm;
4. Thick - over 4 cm.

When giving yourself a lip print and looking at your width you will need to determine and consider what each width is on the top or bottom lip.

Small / thin: tend to keep to themselves, are quiet and courteous. If your lips are small and thin on top you have a lot of self worry about yourself and if your lip is smaller on the bottom than the top you are often worrying about what others think of you.

Thin lower lip shows you are careful with money and numbers. You may also have a tendency to become frugal.

Thin upper lip, reveals you can be considered a perfectionist, and be extremely passionate about subjects that interest you, be mindful of becoming OCD (obsessive compulsive disorder).

Thick / large: A thick top lip would indicate you have a tendency to care for others more than for yourself. You are often mothering or have a motherly tendency. You will worry about everyone else and may put your own needs to the bottom of the care pile. This is something that you will need to mindful of. A great balance can be achieved and allow others to help YOU.

A large bottom lip can make you a great influencer of others and you are more often than not known for being grounded and giving. You are known for keeping secrets and leading your life with a *can do* attitude. If for some reason you tend to stumble and find yourself with feelings of inadequacy it won't be too long before you turn that around with your natural *can do* attitude. You make a great fundraiser and have philanthropic desires.

Full upper lip people are considered to be great listeners and hugely compassionate, whilst full lower lip people are more often generous and creative with their ideas.

Chapter 5

Lip colour
and your energy level

When taking your lip print you will need to look at the intensity and colour of your actual print. If your lip print is full and dense with colour that this indicates that you are full of energy and feeling good with loads of power.

Likewise if when you give yourself a lip print reading the lip print is almost colourless, clear or pale, you are feeling exhausted and running on empty, lacking in energy and feeling quite weak or tired.

You also need to consider after each lip print what your shape looks like. If for example you have a three print lip reading and each print gets bigger and more open, this shows that you are open to new experiences and new ideas.

If, however, it tends to close and get smaller, this shows that you are closed off to whatever life is presenting at the moment to you. It can also indicate a self sabotaging pattern of keeping yourself hidden or small. Often if this is the case you will know that you have been blocking friendships or fun outings that may have given you a new experience.

White lines / spaces: White lines on either the top or the bottom indicate something that you need to communicate to others or perhaps yourself. What this is depends largely where the lines or white spaces are on your lips. For example if you have a lot of white space in the centre of your top lip this will indicate that you need to have a heartfelt chat to someone who is very close to you.

Often it will be a loved one, sibling or other family member to whom you feel you need to express your opinion. You will generally know what this is, as is will regularly pop into your head.

Red lines / spaces: Red lines on either top or bottom indicate your internal self and are based more on emotional and spiritual situations rather than physical and environmental ones.

These lines also tell a story about what you are here to do, or your soul's journey. They indicate what you believe, what you trust and where you are going. They often also show, especially if they are straight without other lines going through them, that you have a clear path to achieve any outcomes you want. When there are other lines going through, this indicates a feeling of being stuck or sabotaging what you know.

Space: If you have a lot of big white spaces this shows disconnection or disbelief in a situation that you may have kept hidden from others. Generally white spaces and lines are reflective of your outside world, such as your physical environment or personal relationships. They can also indicate a physical separation from the situation.

If, however, you have no white spaces this could show stubbornness: you may have a one sided opinion and be unwilling to listen to others. It is similar to "my way or the highway" as the saying goes.

Chapter 6

Lip lines

There are literally a hundred lip lines on your lips.

Lines, can be upper, middle, or bottom.

Upper lip lines: Represent outside, physical and environmental concerns.

Middle lines top and bottom: Represent internal knowing, sometimes indicating things are yet to be expressed by you. You still need to say things around this situation.

Bottom lip lines: Represent what you do or are meant to be doing in this lifetime. This is your soul's path. It's your inner knowing of your greater calling. These lines can also be linked to depression, anxiety, IBS, weight gain or loss. You need to be very mindful of the thick lines present on your lips from the inside out.

Here is a list of the twelve most common lip lines that you will come across. This gives you a great way to begin your own reading.

1. Thick lines: Represent a variety of issues including large gaps in your well being and emotional needs. Often things have been left unspoken or forgotten about but can deeply affect the way we currently feel about ourselves.

2. Thin lines: That are clustered together can equate to a hidden anger that sits deep within. If the lines sit in a sequence and form a single line they express the need to change a lot of physical things that can be happening to you right now. This can also mean little lines that don't go through to the end. It could also serve as a reminder that you start and stop a lot of things.

3. Side lines: Endings or finished with – this can also mean a new beginning.

4. Crisscross lines: Confused about which direction to take. If the lines are red, it's an internal issue and if the lines are white it's more about the physical side of things.

5. Diamond lines: You are creative, artistic and like shiny new things. You like to dramatise stories and love possessions. This can also represent that you are a great listener and are given roles around trust. Be mindful of becoming too attached to your possessions as if you become unbalanced you may be perceived as hoarding or selfish.

6. Crevasses: Show movement in your situation - you are ready to move past this situation. You could be feeling stressed around this and may feel very rigid towards any outcome that is given to you.

7. Scars: Represent a opportunity for new beginnings. You will need to be aware of your personal attitude towards this. You have the chance to move through or stay feeling stuck.

8. Straight: Indicates a clear knowing of where you are going, even if you have not achieved your desired outcome. Be mindful of horizontal lines on your straight lines.

9. Vertical: Not sure what direction you need to take, waiting for inspiration.

10. Horizontal: Can show blocks or a situation that has been finished with.

11. Smudges: Sabotaging and blocking, especially when they are solid red in colour, can appear in either top or bottom lips. Smudging internally shows unknowing or not yet being ready for the next step. You are working on upgrading yourself to the next level of self.

12. Pictures: When focusing on these attributes in a lip reading they will jump out at you and there is no deigning these pictures representing figurines, animals and various other forms. This symbolizes a deep/soul connection and is something that you are destined to do in your life. You should consider all attributes of what the symbol means especially in a metaphysical way.

13. Middle Indent shape: This is best described as the centre of the top of your lip, which I call your heart centre. There are three main types.

Pointy: You are highly creative and have a great sense of humour. People will listen to your message so be mindful of what you say. You also love very deeply and passionately, and are publicly open with who you are loving.

Rounded: You will keep how you love a little bit more protected, and won't be so open to public displays of affection, preferring to keep this to yourself and in private. You offer a rather cool grounded way in your approach to your life. It's calming, not intense and people love you for that. You will find that most people will like you as they find you non-threatening, easy-going and a lot of fun.

Flat: You are a great manifestor, creator and leader, although you will keep these talents mostly to yourself for fear of judgment of others. You are driven and determined to make a difference and are passionate. Your love barometer can be seen as stand-offish or can't be bothered or even understated, yet if people take the time to look within they will find one big hearted person. You have many layers of love that you will keep to yourself and only show the right person to whom you will give 110%.

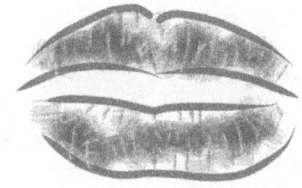

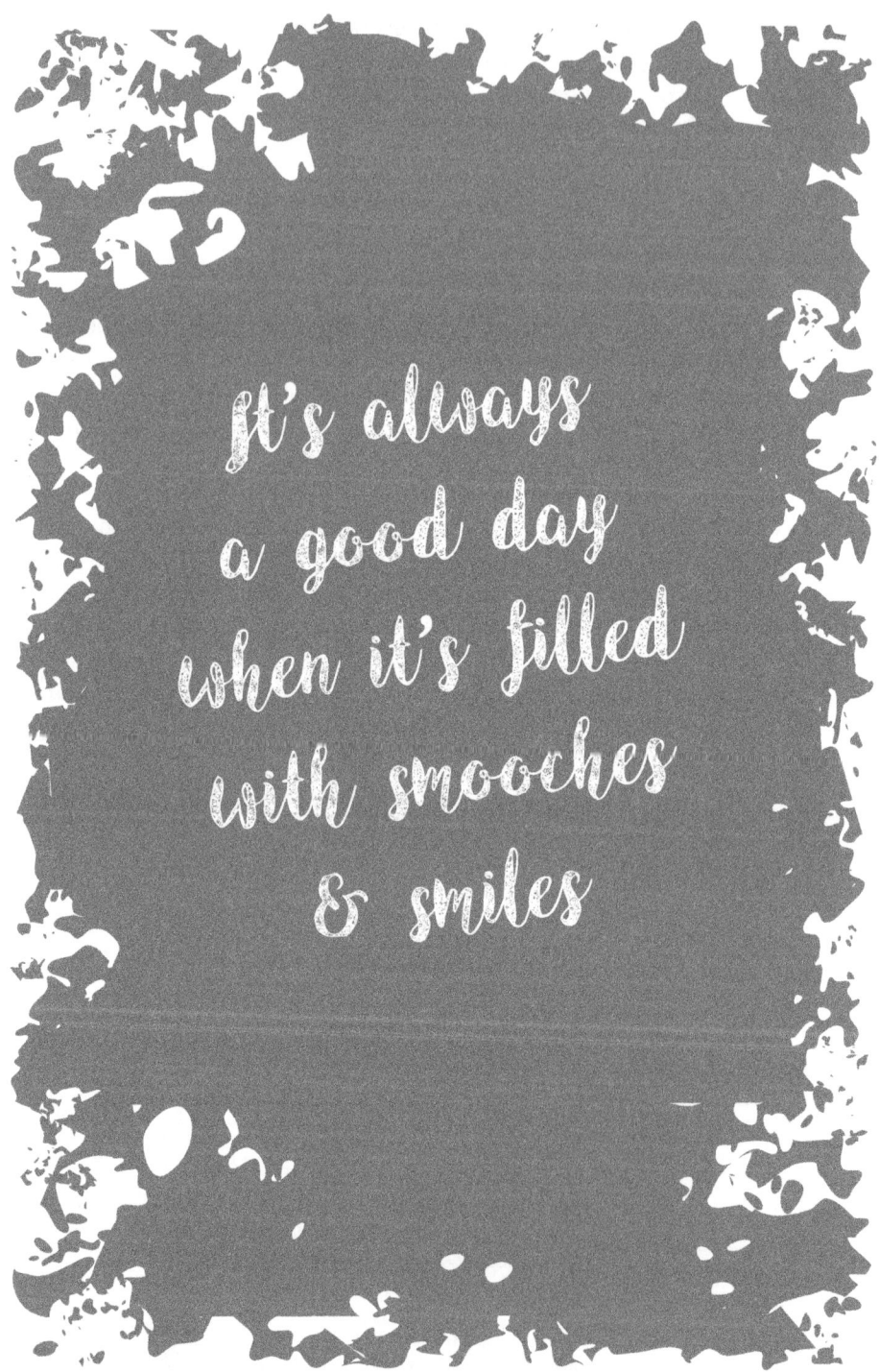

It's always
a good day
when it's filled
with smooches
& smiles

Chapter 7
What your philtrum, bottom lip & side shape means

The philtrum runs from your heart centre at the top of your lip to the centre of the beginning of your nose. The philtrum is responsible for helping you with your expression. Simply looking at the shape, size and width can help you discover more about your personality.

These are the three main areas to take into consideration.

When you have a long, straight and often prominent philtrum, this can represent a sign of stubbornness or perhaps someone who likes things orderly. You love rules and regulations and thrive on anything that is tidy and systematic. You may have a tendency to want to help others find order in their lives. Being mindful that not everyone thinks like you is something to consider, or you could seem too forceful.

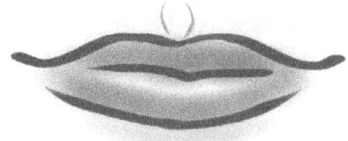

If you have a short philtrum this can often mean that you have a short fuse. As a living soul, you can become quite passionate about certain projects that you do. Often anything that you put your mind to will be successful. Be careful not to step on people's toes or be too bossy.

Having a wide philtrum means you are open to new experiences and may be called a party person. You could be described as a being playful, a hipster, creative and a visionary. You're the big picture kind of person. Driven and determined to make changes. You are often positive, funny and witty. Your challenge is to listen to what others are saying as you can get carried away within your own thoughts.

What's your bottom lip arch meaning all about?

Your lip arch plays a significant role in how the world sees you, which is different from how you see and treat yourself from your top lip. A bottom lip arch is best described as the small or large indent that sits directly in the middle and protrudes from the bottom lip area.

The bottom arch represents generosity and how the world sees it in you. If for example you have a wide and deep arch you would be considered to be very generous. If on the other hand you have a small and very shallow arch you may be seen as more cautious with your giving.

There is nothing wrong with either; it is merely the way you are perceived by the world on an intuitive level. People with no arch often keep things to themselves and make great secret keepers because they value "self and privacy". Whereas a person with a large deep and bottom arch may like to talk and share (it's the giving thing they do) and accidentally give away your secrets.

The saying "Loose lips sink ships" comes to mind

A large, very wide and deep bottom arch person may be predisposed to leaving things wide open and talking ten to the dozen. These attributes can also help people trust them more, yet you may have to consider that they may not always tell the truth and can often over exaggerate and suffer from verbal dribble.

Downturned or upturned sides or flat

Have you ever considered the different styles of the sides or corners of your mouth and why some people may have a mouth that hangs down whilst others look like they wear a permanent smile? Or corners that are straight? What is it with the different styles?

If for example your mouth corners appear to be in a straight line, then you might be thought of as being straight laced or a 'goody-two-shoes'. This also means that you make a great counsellor as you can sit right in the middle of any situation and see both sides, be non-biased.

Having a straight cornered mouth means you are also very spiritually connected and a grounded character and are deeply connected to the earth. You'll love all things that nature has to offer.

On the other hand, if the corner of your mouth is permanently smiley, you will more often than not be the joker or see the funny side of things. You could even be known as the class clown or person who plays harmless funny jokes on others. Your chosen career would be somewhere more light hearted and somewhere where being funny and witty could win you favours, such as a customer service representative, waitress, bartender, sporting, holidaying fun projects. Anywhere that enables you to lighten up the mood.

However, if your mouth corners face down you'll be better known for seeing the worst in any situation, and you would be best described as a pessimist. This doesn't make you a sad person but you will naturally see the worst possible situation. You also like order and love fixing things that are 'not working'.

Over crowding, money, waste and pollution are your grievances. You make a great system analyser, judge, or someone of authority, leading the way to 'save the world'.

Why read
your mind
when you can
read
your lips

Chapter 8

Stories of lip print readings

All lip print reading clients' names have been changed for privacy reasons.

The best thing about lip print reading is that it is different to other ways of finding out more about your life and wellbeing on an intuitive level. I love doing this type of reading because it is a lot of fun and unlike any other reading your lip print can change from hour to hour depending on what's on your mind at the time.

Every reading is different and offers a unique experience to the person receiving it. I suggest having a lip print reading at the change of each season or at least twice a year.

They are also a lot of fun and many clients learn a great deal more about themselves as a result of investing in a lip print reading.

The concept of lip print readings is based on an ancient practice dating back more than 3000 years, when it was a diagnostic tool used by traditional Chinese medicine practitioners and other healing therapists to help their clients.

SALLY'S STORY
Recognising Love

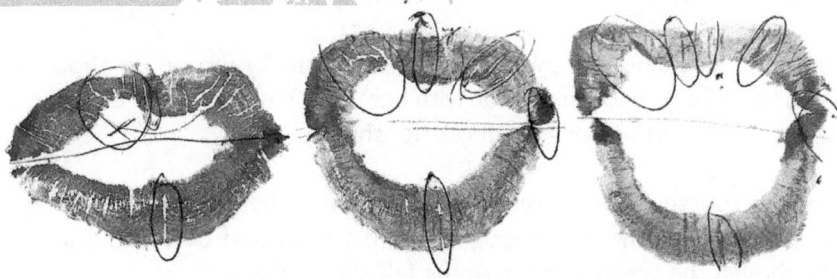

Sally's lip print reading was a journey back into her life and love. The first thing that I noticed when I looked at Sally's print was a big gap around her high heart, as if she was missing love or had lost trust in what love was, and didn't recognise it or what she could be missing. She had also blocked out a lot of possibilities for love in her past by the deep red and solid lines that were present on her lip print.

Sally had spent her life learning and studying and taking care of others and even though she was practising being kind to herself, her lips showed me that she had some major blocks around this particular subject. Uncovering them and being able to suggest simple solutions would be key to her being able to move forward.

Seeing Sally's spiritual and grounded path I knew her connection to her soul path was a deep one. Yet the gap indicated above on her top lip told me another story.

Sally was raised in an era that saw her mother go to church on a regular basis and she had always been mindful and respectful of what she was taught as a young girl. When she was younger Sally had fallen deeply in love with a young man from a different country.

When the two wished to get married, the problems appeared. Should he choose to marry Sally, it would mean that he would not be able to remain part of his family, who would not allow Sally to convert to his spiritual belief.

Sally, who was always thinking of others, didn't want her love to be estranged from his family and so she chose to leave him. These were the actions deeply set in Sally's memories and beliefs about herself.

For although Sally chose love, her sweetheart chose his family. Deep down Sally had always thought that she wasn't good enough and felt rejected by love. Even though her decision to leave was completely hers, she had hoped that he would choose their love.

This had tested Sally and even though she eventually moved on, those feelings of not being good enough still sat with her. Sally never married or had children despite being in other long-term relationships.

Over the course of the lip reading Sally revealed that she was still living in her previous partner's house although they had separated over five years before. Even though she wanted to move she felt she couldn't.

This left her holding on to things that didn't serve her purpose any more, and indeed were weighing her down with being unable to make the call to leave the house. She had spent the last five years researching, learning and studying and felt it was time to vacate her ex-partner's house.

This realisation of not being able to let things go came back to her feelings of being abandoned from her first love, the one whom she never really wanted to leave, but was forced to by circumstances.

It became clear that Sally was really holding on to her old love, and had carried these feelings of not being good enough most of her adult life, because her young beau had chosen his family instead of running away with her.

These feelings were deeply etched in Sally's psyche, hidden from most of the world except her own secret heart. Sally needed to be given the tools on how to let go and move forward so that she could indeed find her soul mate, who I could see was waiting for her. And her new career would thrive, but first taking care of Sally needed to be the first priority.

It was suggested that Sally really started to treat herself, and even though she did practise this on a regular basis I needed to shift her way of thinking of doing something until something or someone else came along. I began to suggest different ways that Sally could treat herself and was guided to propose the '101 ways to take care of Sally'. These treats were to become second nature and couldn't be of a materialistic nature.

Sally was asked to be creative and indulge in kind words, to write letters to the people she had loved and give herself forgiveness messages everyday.

When something or someone triggers a deep belief that you're not good enough or when you feel abandoned or unloved, sometimes even though you know you did the right thing at the time, the feeling can sometimes sit with you without your even recognising it.

You often end up with a sense of not being good enough that will keep you feeling stuck for almost a life time. It was Sally's desire to move from her ex-partner's house that triggered these motionless responses to herself.

Sally finally got that she had never let go of her one true love despite thinking she had.

Once Sally finds her way to being able to forgive herself for unconsciously keeping her stuck, there is room to move forward and find her passion and purpose and perhaps her soul mate.

A LITTLE BOOK ABOUT LIPS

Angels of Love

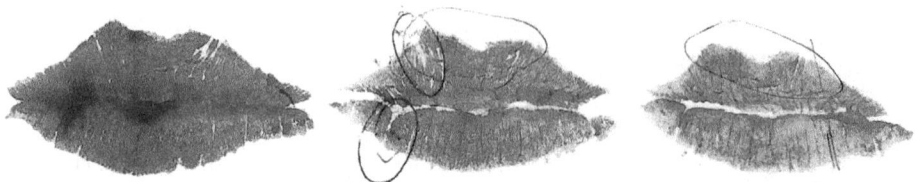

Elizabeth's reading was probably one of the hardest readings I have ever done, due to a recent death. I could sense her sadness. She had lost her husband of 40+ years who had been her soul mate and her entire life. He was a magnificent man who adored his family and wife.

Elizabeth's lip print indicated she had shut herself off from the world although I could see she passionately loved people by her generous and rounded heart centre. There was a sense of deep regret and guilt around her husband's passing, as she never got to say goodbye.

Her lip print shows a rectangular shape, so for Elizabeth everything needs to be in order and in its place.

As I read the lip print reading I began to understand more about the absolute guilt that she was suffering from because she wasn't present when he passed away.

Understanding this situation as a gift and not a burden, I needed Elizabeth to understand the precious legacy she had allowed her husband as he passed. It was revealed he had not wanted her to be present during his final moments and had waited till she had left the room and was with other family members before taking his final breath.

By talking with Elizabeth I knew I had to help her understand her husband's final wishes. Just around her communication area there were many gaps, which generally indicates that there are things that need to be said or something that you want to say to someone, even after the person has passed away.

By sharing some really unique ways of communicating with her husband I helped Elizabeth to be able to begin to establish different ways in which she could have the conversation she so desperately wanted.

Teaching Elizabeth how to keep in touch with her husband and specifically asking for signs that he was with her which she could easily understand would help with her transition into new beginnings.

Angels are very responsive to your questions and only want to help you. Beginning conversations with passed loved ones is a strong way to heal the empty feeling, especially if you have been the one caring for them.

By connecting with different techniques this truly helps the process of grief begin to heal. Allowing these conversations to take place enables you to move through the different stages of heartache and loss.

Elizabeth had a gorgeous creative side to her which she was about to rediscover. During our lip reading it was suggested that any form of artwork would be deeply healing for her. Therfore she would find great peace and new inspiration from taking classes that involved her in thinking creatively.

With new beginnings it's important to establish a new routine and to be brave and discover different things about yourself. When going through this transition its important to recognise the little gifts of friendship and communication.

Writing letters to loved ones that have passed is a great way to say your goodbyes, especially if you feel there are things left unsaid between you. By doing these little yet very important rituals, especially if you work with the moon cycles, will help you start your new beginnings and feel at peace with where your life is right now.

A new moon is great for bringing in new ideas and new ways, as a full moon is great for letting go of the things that no longer serve you. Depending on your personal situation you can work the moons to suit you.

After writing letters it's important to let them go into the atmosphere. A simple way to do this is by burning them under the respective moon that you choose. This can work with anything that you desire and is very powerful.

DANIELLE'S STORY
Finding Feminine

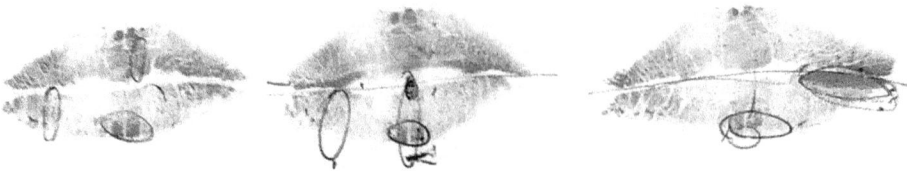

Do you ever wonder why you do the things you do? Are you clean and tidy or a little messy and a bit creative. With lip print readings there is no hiding from "who" you are.

Danielle works in an office and loves order, being highly organised and controlling everything.

She loves supporting people with their own ideas and keeping things precise. Looking at Danielle's lip print I could see that she had a lot of crisscross and sideways lines around the personal power section of her top lip. It was as though she had been challenged about believing in herself.

Interestingly Danielle was a smoker many years ago and although she no longer smoked the anger and communication suppression was still prevalent on her lips.

Smoking is mostly related to anger or suffocation of love. It's also about control of the things you can't control.

Through the reading we had established that she had considered her brother to be the favourite because he was the only boy in her family growing up and as a young girl she believed her father favoured him.

Still today she had taken on a more masculine role as she wasn't really into feminine things; even her job provided the main income into the family household. And although Danielle loved her career and wasn't burdened by her responsibilities she had forgotten to nurture her female essence.

Danielle normally just gets out of bed, throws on the things closest, and generally roams around making things neat and perfect for everyone else. The order of everything is wonderful especially when it comes to others. She loved to focus on other things.

The lip print showed a block around her lower lip with a heavy smudge mark, which often indicates a reluctance to be sexually active or if you are, appreciating and having fun with it.

"Can you just hurry up" are the words we used to describe her reluctance? Perhaps you relate to this?

By blocking her sexuality, she had indeed forgotten her own desires of being feminine, more than likely because of her deep belief that her brother was considered the favourite. It was a memory that was embedded.

Retraining the way you think and starting to create little ways in which you can be unique and feminine can be a really fun way to gain your womanly self back.

Whilst Danielle was listening we began to laugh as it was only that morning that she had picked up some jewellery and considered wearing it. When the time came to wear it she reconsidered as she couldn't be bothered.

'After all who's looking anyway?' was how she was thinking. Bringing attention to her feminine self was something she didn't enjoy.

By introducing fun things such as jewellery, candles and maybe even a skirt or a pair of fancy shoes or perhaps a bracelet that could help her feel more feminine would start to heal the long held belief that she wasn't liked because she was female.

Although this could only be a perception, it is still Danielle's belief that her father liked her brother more. Slowly introducing one thing at a time that represents her female self is a great way to begin to rethink her childhood memories.

Try doing something feminine for yourself, not because people are looking or not looking. Simply for yourself. It's a big lesson and one I'm sure as you get better at it will give you immense enjoyment.

Try doing these things to help you embrace your soul self

- Taking a long bubble bath
- Using essential oils
- Wearing colourful underwear
- Using a little colourful lip balm
- Making earrings

There are so many things that we unconsciously carry into adulthood from our childhood. If you begin to take the little daily steps, even if it's on a physical level, it is the start to understanding more about situations.

Section Four   The language of your lips

Chapter 1

What your words mean

Think about how these words make you feel:

Love words: adore, crush, cherish, respect, passion, love, romance, relationship, desire, hope, longing, yearning, admire, treasure, fondness, affection.

Power: influence, strong, capable, able, yes, potential, pull, rule, resourceful, prestige, inspire.

Wisdom: clever, wise, perceptive, knowing, intuition, smart, sense, uncanny, experienced, sophistication, informative.

Hate: hostile, antagonism, repulsed, bitter, bad blood, malice, loathing.

Swear words: idiot, shit, arsehole, bloody, bitch, cow, God, Jesus Christ, pissed off, bullshit, f#*k, c#*t, bastard, dickhead, knob, mother f#*^*r, prick, w%*ker.

Condolence and sad words: heartache, sorrow, sadness, sad, gloom, melancholy, pain, mourning, suffering, heartbreak.

Happy words: thrilled, joy, glad, blessed, grateful, contented, delighted, happy, merry, cheerful, spirited, energised, vibrant, fortunate, hilarious, laughter, optimistic, animated,

Romantic words: dreamy, loving, charming, rapturous, wooing, doting, devoted, have a crush on, hot.

Have you ever really stopped and thought about the power of the words that you use?

Did you know that each word carries a vibrational energy that sets the tone for what you are saying and how you are saying it? Every word you use to describe yourself or someone else can make someone feel happy or sad.

Every cell in your entire body holds a little memory box that remembers things that you do and say. These cells are responsible for how you feel, based on the vibration and feelings of those words.

Our bodies are made of 12 different systems, one of which is the Central Nervous System or CNS. It's responsible for taking nutrients and our feelings and emotions to all the different parts of our bodies. It is the Central Nervous System that is responsible for our emotional well being.

I tend to think of this as own unique little village and road map, with an entire team of builders, delivery and transport companies, chefs, cleaners, nurses, personal trainers, coaches, electricians, doctors, journalists, web designers, coders, graphic artists, bloggers. Every single one has an important role to do.

It's got roundabouts, traffic lights, red flags, signs, horns, bells and the odd whistle or two to navigate throughout our entire system.

Your lips have on average 10,000 nerve endings and yet the area is only around 3mm thick. This makes your lip area the most sensitive part of your body.

And it is of particular importance as it is responsible for so many things. The mouth is the start of the digestive system, responsible for allowing food to enter your stomach.

Your mouth is also important because it allows us to communicate with others. There is one universal sign, your smile, that despite any language or cultural background is recognised as a form of greeting.

Think about this for a moment. No other part of your body has responsibility like your mouth and it is the one area that is keeping you alive, feeding and nurturing you.

With this in mind, when you use words that make you feel sad about the way you look or how your lips look, it's sending messages throughout your body telling every other cell that something is wrong.

Think about a conversation you've had with one of your friends about your lips; was it a positive or a negative one?

Did you say something like; "Oh if only I didn't have so many lines around my top lip" or perhaps you expressed how you don't like your thin top lip and are thinking of having injectables to fix your perceived problem?

This sends up a red flag to the body, and immediately your cells begin to take a sad and unhappy memory of your words. When you keep saying this, it becomes ingrained so that every time you think about that problem you immediately feel sad or deprived.

The next time you begin to start to think like this, why not change it around and help your body feel happier by giving it a positive word instead of a negative word. You'll be surprised at how quickly your body likes being positive and happy.

You can do this really simply by saying out loud or to yourself fun, happy and positive words, by asking your body to make you aware every time you say something that is negative about yourself and replace it with a positive word. It's really that easy!

When you begin to do this you will become very mindful of the words you use and the power behind them.

If you are still not convinced that words matters, start listening to other people's conversation and start to see if they are happy, angry or sad. You could also watch their body language. Are they laughing and engaging in conversation, or yelling and looking intense?

By doing this you will begin to learn more about vibrational energy and feelings and what it does to our bodies. I suggest you play with words in every conversation you have and see how you feel. Keep a diary of what words you use every day and write the feelings you have at the end of each day. You might just be surprised at the different results you have.

What ever you do, remember you are a work in progress and don't beat yourself up if you end up having a bad day full of swear words and negativity. Because it's when you become aware that you can start to make positive changes in your world.

Why not have a word a day that you use and a word a day that you don't use. That way you can be your own personal word coach. Most importantly, have fun with it.

Chapter 2
Mindfulness matters

As humans we are conditioned to think that the only way to learn or believe in something is by seeing it; "seeing is believing" is a familiar phrase. Yet there is one thing in the entire world that we all desire to experience and have, yet we can never touch it, see it or buy it. That is LOVE!

As we evolve and learn more about the environment that we live in, it's important to remember what our ancestors thought. Such as the world was flat, the earth was the centre of the universe, and there were only nine planets in our solar system.

What we now know and take for granted is that the world is round, there are many other galaxies in our universe and Pluto is now a dwarf planet

I believe that one day our education systems will teach about vibrational energy, feelings and emotions as they teach maths and science today.

When it comes to love or that feeling of love nothing else matters. Think about this for a moment. It's the one thing you can't pop to the shops and pick up. Imagine saying to your friend or partner; "Hey honey, can you pick me up a box of love. It's in aisle five right beside the teabags. Oh can you get me the red box it feels so much better than the yellow one we had last time."

Now as silly as this sounds, it's true you can't buy love, you can't touch it, pick it up and smell it. You can only ever feel it. It's important to understand why the love vibe is so meaningful to us.

As humans this 'love stuff' is about feeling happy and good about ourselves. It's a genuine surge of electricity and energy running through our bodies. When this doesn't happen it is more likely that you will suffer from an imbalance or disease. You'll get angry and down on yourself, feel unworthy of many things and focus on the things you don't have and want rather than the things you already have.

You tend to think about physical and material things more than yourself and can often fill your world with stuff or keep things way too long. Does that sound familiar?

Keeping this in mind, feeling good and being able to see the good in yourself is something most people struggle with. Often as givers and nurturers we forget to focus on ourselves, believing this is selfish.

You spend all your time caring for others, seeing the beauty and kindness in everyone except yourself.

This I believe is a direct result of what we think about ourselves. When is the last time you considered yourself beautiful? You can easily see it in others yet struggle to see it in yourself. Which words do you use to describe yourself?

Fun, happy, kind, generous or witty? How do your friends describe you? How do you describe your friends?

Or perhaps you fill your words with; I wish I had her lips, teeth, boobs & butt. I hate my stumpy frumpy legs, arms. I really don't like my neck; it's too short, I want a long neck like whoever.

Taking this into consideration you probably have all of these things already, you just can't see them for yourself.

Living in the "love vibe" is a really simple concept to understand and becoming more mindful of what you think is a great place to start.

Simply be gracious to yourself, be responsible for yourself and stop blaming others for where your life is right now. Your love vibe is yours to own.

I believe it's important to be kind to yourself and work on the notion that everything that presents in your life is for you to learn from. Being mindful of this is the first step if you choose!

Having the 'love vibe' is an empowering movement that you do with yourself. And recognising the difference between love (which is your heart) and ego (which is your mind).

Your heart tells you all the things that you're great at and should do, and the ego is the little voice that tells you all the things you can't or shouldn't do, the things you're not good at or don't deserve; it's the drama in your life.

It's up to you to learn how to appreciate both of these things. Because as you become aware of what the ego is saying you shouldn't do, this is where you get the most growth in your mindfulness quest. It's the friction between the heart and the ego that makes the mindfulness growth happen.

In case you are wondering, beauty is energy. It's a vibe and the more you understand this about yourself the more likely your mindfulness will take a step up in the right direction.

It's when you feel at peace with yourself and what you will attract more of in your life.

It's
all about
the vibe
in your words,
use your words
for good

Chapter 3

Throw-away words and changing bad habits

How many times a day do you throw your words away with comments telling yourself, *"I hate my hair, I hate my lips, my butt's too big, I'm so stupid, you're a idiot, you're dumb, I wish I had better teeth"*?

The more times you repeat these the more likely it is that you will truly begin to feel worth-less.

The habit of swearing and using foul language has been used across all time in history. It's also been scientifically proven that swearing and saying curse words raises your heart rate and can increase resistance to pain. Perhaps that's why we naturally use a cuss word when we hurt ourselves.

Likewise there have been many studies that indicate the power between negative and positive words.

Have you ever walked past someone who has been behaving badly, swearing?

Or been on the receiving end where we've had feelings of being shamed, humiliated, dismissed, belittled or criticised. I'm sure you'll agree it's not a nice way to feel.

Most people use negative and swear words to express anger, emotions or frustration. We can also use them in humorous situations or even to harass and bully someone. It's also a sign of disrespect, inflated ego and showing off.

With that in mind, when you use words that are negative, hurtful and disrespectful to yourself or others it's not surprising that we can feel powerful when saying them or feel disgusting and worthless when receiving them.

I believe that when we get nervous, scared or live in fear we use these words more often than we should. For me I see it as a sign of protecting the imbalance and detracting from the fear that sits directly in your heart.

Have you ever wondered why your lip can quiver when you are scared, cold, nervous or feeling like you're going to cry? That's because directly in the centre of your top lip is your heart centre, which is responsible for keeping you safe, loved and nurtured.

Think about this for a moment. When you go to touch something hot or sip a hot cup of coffee or tea, where do you immediately put it to your lip to feel if it's safe to consume. To your top lip, *right?*

If you are feeling distressed you begin to step into your fear and ego, and this is when you are more likely to feel like you are losing control of something or someone, and start to swear and use negative words to elevate your heart rate and decrease the feelings on your skin. It's commonly referred to as *fight or flight.*

However, with that said, you must remember the negativity of the words used and the intent behind them. Even when you're swearing in a fun and jovial way it's still releasing a negative energy, especially to those for whom it's intended and who are receiving it.

We never really think that sound and vibration travel through our energy field on a physical level. Considering that we are around 80% water and sound vibrations have been proven to travel through water four times faster than air, it's no wonder we feel so deeply connected and affected by words. Especially the throw-away ones that we don't consider to be hurtful.

The more often you hear and use negative words, the more likely you are to continue to use them. It becomes a pattern just like learning your times table when you went to school.

You should become aware that your throw-away words matter and can leave a direct impact on your entire body, in particular your lip area because it's the most sensitive and one of the thinnest parts of your body.

Try turning your words around and start saying, *"I am, I can, I like, I love"*. It's an easy way to start.

Have a gratitude jar and everyday write something amazing about yourself on a sticky note and put in the jar.

Start a diary and fill it with affirmations of positivity.

Reward yourself every time you choose a positive word instead of a negative one.

- Avoid gossiping.

- Stop the self-criticism.

- Wear colourful clothes.

Remember your feelings matter as much as other people's feelings do, so considering this, be mindful of how you speak to yourself and others. Start to make that positive change in your life.

Surround yourself with positive uplifting people and things to do. Make simple goals to be more aware of just how powerful your words are.

A LITTLE BOOK ABOUT LIPS

One
little kiss
can make
a difference

Chapter 4

The secret to kissing

Did you know that each year on July 6th there is an entire day dedicated to kissing? This is the perfect time to celebrate all things loving about you and your lips.

But there's more to a kiss than you might think; have you ever had that awkward moment when you end up actually connecting your lips with a complete stranger's lips when you meant to kiss them on the cheek? Doesn't it tend to leave you feeling embarrassed?

Kissing is one of the most loving things we do, whether it's a friendly kiss on the cheek with a friend or a heart warming expression of your love with someone special. We've all had a memorable kiss that can 'literally take your breath away', or leave you feeling like you've been kissed by yet another frog.

This universal language of love and friendship is an eco system of expression and given that we now know our lips are the most sensitive part of our body perhaps this is why it's yet another way, similar to your smile, that we can express ourselves without talking.

Equally the way we kiss or are being kissed can be an explanation of how we know someone and how we want them to know us.

Here are my 12 favourite kissing styles all wrapped up

Friendship kiss: Also known as the greeting hello kiss. Generally, on either side of your face and rarely on your lips. The touching of the cheeks pays reference to trust and self worth. And this style of kissing is generally found to be an appropriate way to greet people you are familiar with but not intimate with. It's about you wanting them to trust and like you. However you generally don't give a stranger a kiss like this the first time you meet them. Most people will start with a hand shake but as you get more familiar with them you will lead with a greeting kiss on the cheek as you leave whether it's the opposite sex or two females.

Forehead kiss: This represents a deep connection and fondness with who you are. Gentle, kind and loving. You have a more intimate connection with this person. Often it's a sign of inner wisdom and healing. The forehead kiss is a common way to kiss your children as they grow up and also your partner. It's very unlikely that you would kiss a stranger or an acquaintance on the head, especially at a business/networking meeting.

French kiss: This is an intimate event shared between two people who have loving and deep affectionate feelings towards each other. It's the most intimate way to express your feelings to someone you care about. The lips are connected to every chakra point, particularly the heart chakra.

Grandmother kiss: Grandmothers can get away with absolutely anything. She'll come in and just grab you in a big hug, look you straight on and give you a kiss on each side of your cheeks.

Sometimes, she might even grab your face while she's doing it.

There are no rules for getting out of a grandmother kiss and you will have to accept it whether you are two, 22 or 52 years of age.

Air kiss: This is a Beverly Hills housewives-type kiss. They will make the noise, but there is no connection.

What this is saying is that they really want the other person to like them, but they are setting boundaries so they don't get too close.

They might choose to have a proper friendship kiss in a less public setting, but the air kiss is all about image and the way in which they want to be perceived.

Eye kiss: This is really gentle, kind and tender. You have a more intimate relationship with that person and it is usually used for husbands or lovers.

You can also use this on a child such as kissing their eyes if they are feeling hurt or tired.

It shows an intimate connection with them. You really adore that person.

Hand kissing: Often a desired greeting for an upper class gentleman meeting an equally upper class lady in a formal setting. The classic hand kiss is not common today but dates back to the eighteenth and nineteenth centuries. It was the way to greet a lady to whom the gentleman wished to show great respect. Hand shaking was considered bad taste. However, the lady must first present her hand. If she didn't, then a simple bow of the head would be sufficient.

Neck kiss: Gives the recipient an all so gorgeous tingly sensation. This shouldn't be confused with a love bite or hickie as the common phrase is. A kiss on the neck, especially at the back is soft, and incredibly sensual. Often given to/by someone who wants to impress you.

Quick kiss: This quickie is generally for the familiar or a parent. This is where the connection of the lips is made yet only for a second or two. Generally, how you may say hello or goodbye to a partner. Or to kiss a young child good night.

Peck: This is the quickie where you may not even actually connect the lips. When you use the 'peck kiss' you will be more familiar with the person, generally a partner or a loved one

Top of head: A beautiful deep sign of affection and often carried out between a father and a daughter. Kissing on the top of your head has a deep connection with your inner wisdom and your connection to the crown chakra. How you're viewed or being viewed to your higher self.

Awkward kiss: When you go to shake hands and/or cheek-kiss a person with whom you are not familiar. You may end up going to the same side as the person you're about to kiss. This could mean a sign of subconscious attraction. Or that you are actually kissing a left handed person. The rule of thumb when it comes to kissing is that you should lean towards the non dominant or feminine side to kiss.

You define your feminine side as the side you don't write with. Mostly it is to the left.

Kisser tips

When kissing or greeting someone to say hello always go to the non-dominant side of the face/body. This is usually the left hand side; I say 'keep left to avoid a head on'.

A LITTLE BOOK ABOUT LIPS

Keep a diary
and play
with your words
in every
conversation

Section Five   Lip care and treatments

Chapter 1

Recipes

Lip Mask - Diva delish

Raw cacao, cinnamon and honey

Mix ½ teaspoon of each into a small bowl and apply to lip area. Leave on for 5 minutes; then rinse and apply a good quality fragrance-free balm.

These ingredients are well known as mild and effective stimulants and will help increase blood flow to the area and smooth it out.

Lip exfoliation - Strawberry Kisses

2 tablespoons of fresh mint, ½ teaspoon of ground ginger, and 1 strawberry and a ¼ teaspoon of orange rind.

Mix altogether in a blender and apply to lip area. Use circular motions above and below for even better effects. Rinse off and apply a good balm.

Lip collagen boost - Smocha smooch

1 teaspoon of ground organic coffee, ½ teaspoon of raw cacao, 1 teaspoon of oats, 2 teaspoons of pure vanilla extract. Rub into lips and leave on for 5 -10 minutes before rinsing off.

This a great way to boost the collagen in your lips and contains on average per 100 gr 30 grams of protein - a fantastic way to restore the collagen.

Lip bleed - Lush-lippy

Your lipstick feathers or bleeds largely due to your lips being dehydrated. This mask should certainly help ease the symptoms.

2 teaspoons of fresh aloe gel, ½ teaspoon of green tea powder and 2 slices of fresh green cucumber. Blend together and leave on lip area for 10 minutes. Rinse and apply makeup as usual.

Remove flackey skin - Smooth and sooth

1teaspoon of chia seed, 3 to 4 teaspoons of apple cider vinegar, 1/4-1/2 teaspoon of bicarbonate of soda

Mix together to form paste (it will bubble and froth a little). Leave for 10 mins then apply to lip area and massage and leave for approx 3-5 mins. Rinse and apply a good balm.

This helps to remove flakey skin around your lip area.

All of these ingredients are anti-bacterial – anti-viral and anti-inflammatory and can help stop the virus from spreading or getting worse.

Remedies

It's essential with any of these remedies that you drink water.

Wind burn

Use 1 whole black teabag and 1 -2 teaspoons of apple cider vinegar blend. Soak tea bag in vinegar and place on affected lip area as required.

The black tea bag contains tannins that are effective in drawing out the heat whilst the vinegar will relieve the pain and itching.

Cold sores

Use a 1-2 pure vanilla bean mixed with 1 tablespoon of honey and 1 teaspoon of apple cider vinegar. Blend together and apply directly to affected area as soon as you begin to feel the tingly sensation.

Cracks and cuts

It's important to remember to avoid certain foods and products that could make this condition worse. Avoid using things with coffee, cinnamon, camphor and essential oils. And avoid lipsticks and toothpaste.

1 teaspoon of natural yoghurt, 1 teaspoon of turmeric, 1 teaspoon of pure vitamin E.

Blend together and leave on lips for 30 minutes at a time.

Using traditional natural ingredients, can be a great alternative to using commercial products with synthetic chemicals

A LITTLE BOOK ABOUT LIPS

Kissing
and smiling
is the
universal
language of love

Chapter 2

Crushing the secret code on cracked lips

You may not be aware that there are some common natural oils that can cause your lips to feel even worse, especially in winter. One of the main reasons is that during this season your lips are exposed to extreme weather including artificial heating, wind and dry winter conditions.

Here's a list of my top Three crackers to avoid

Coconut oil: Even though this amazing oil is considered a super food in its natural form it may not be the best to apply to your lips, *why?* There's a little known scientific fact about this oil which is that it is a known **comodogenic**; this means it can cause your skin to clog, which creates the perfect atmosphere, especially around your lips, for dryness, acne, pimples and skin irritation to occur. It may be wise to simply eat it instead.

Petroleum Jelly/ mineral oil: Is manufactured from crude oil and although this oil does not penetrate the skin easily, it can cause it to naturally stop any moisture from entering the skin. These oil molecule structures bind other fat soluble vitamins and oils together and take them unabsorbed out of the body, which can produce symptoms of dry and irritated skin.

Undercover names to avoid on labels:
- **Paraffin wax**
- **Benzene**
- **Toluene**
- **PEG**
- **DEA**
- **MEA**
- **Phenoxyethanol.**

Vitamin E: Or tocopheryl acetate is a synthetic version (of vitamin E) made in a laboratory to produce a cheaper by-product. This vitamin or tocopheryl is mixed with acetate (an acid) which can be harmful and cause your skin to become dry and red. It can attack the skin and cause allergic reactions. Stick with the real stuff if you are going to use this.

Undercover names to avoid on labels:
- **Vitamin E acetate**
- **D-alpha-tocopherol**
- **D-alpha-tocopherol acetate.**

What's my secret code lip cracking tip?

To eliminate the feeling of cracked and dry lips look for balms that are **humectant**, which means they offer protection and form a barrier on your lip area whilst being able to reduce the loss of moisture and allow other oils, waxes and butters to penetrate and be absorbed by the body.

Chapter 3

Kiss your cracked lips goodbye five-day challenge

Let's face it, there is nothing worse than having extremely painful, cracked and dry lips, especially when even smiling hurts.

What you may not be aware of is how important your lip ecosystem is to your entire well being. If your lips are continually dry and you want to get some help why not try these super easy lip tips to alleviate the pain and get your lips back on track and healthy again.

INGREDIENTS TO AVOID	WHY
Long stay lip colour	Dehydrates your lips
Salty foods	Dehydrate
Sun	Dehydrates
Essential oils	Not designed to be consumed
Parabens	Hormone disruptor
Mineral Oils	Hormone disruptor
Fragrances	Carcinogenic and hormone disruptors
Benzoin	Causes allergies
Triclosan	Environmental toxin and doesn't break down, also known hormone disruptor
Retyinyl Palmitate	Synthetic form of Vitamin A – which may cause birth defects
D&C 22	Known carcinogen & synthetically derived
Formaldehyde	Known carcinogen & synthetically derived
Synthetics dyes	Contain 3000-5000 chemicals. Manufactures don't have to divulge as it's trademark law
Methyl & Propyl Paraben	Derived from petroleum - known skin irritant and carcinogen
D&C 36	Known carcinogen and synthetically derived
Phthates	Hormone disruptor & carcinogen. Look for DEP, DBP, DEHP & fragrances

FIVE To DO's

1. Drink plenty of water.
2. Use a natural lip protector such as a good lip balm.
3. Eat lots of good healthy greens.
4. Make sure you smile often as it releases happy hormones into your entire body.
5. Take daily care of your lips.

Try following these five tips for just five days - you'll be surprised at how much of a difference it makes to both your lips and your general well being.

Chapter 4

Lip surgery and cosmetic procedures

Did you know that there's been entire industry created with a huge ground swell of users since the early 1990s, largely because people are unhappy with the way they look, particularly with their lips?

I'm talking about the increase in lip injections. Although this is considered relatively safe you must be aware that there is always risk with everything you do.

For me I like to know what and where it has come from before I even think about using anything.

With so many people flocking to get their lips done there are staggering results that suggest people are truly unhappy with the way their lips look.

Let's take a closer look: According to plasticsurgery.org since 2015 there has been a lip augmentation done every 20 minutes, which is an increase by nearly 48% since the year 2000.

Unfortunately, this statistic shows no signs of slowing down. My concern is the underlying reasoning behind so many people, mostly women, getting their lips altered or enhanced.

This medical breakthrough has been used to assist people with medical conditions like access sweating and cerebral palsy, just to name a couple of conditions, as it stops the nerve endings from connecting with each other.

This is the predominant reason why it's so popular within the beauty and cosmetic Industry. It gets delivered in very small amounts injected just under the skin, with most treatments lasting for approximately 4-6 months.

However, what you may not know is that what is being injected is the world's deadliest toxin, the same toxin that is found in food poisoning, although it is heavily diluted, which is just as well as in its pure form it would only take 500 grams (one pound) of this stuff to kill every human on Earth.

Bacterium Clostridium Botulinum type A is found in the stomachs of decaying cows. This toxin works so well because it blocks the central nervous system from communicating. It stops the muscles and central nervous system from becoming over active.

If you remember earlier in the book I spoke to you about the importance of the central nervous system and its effects on your entire body, including your lips.

Have you ever wondered why only doctors and registered nurses can administer these injections?

Bacterium Clostridium Botulinum type A is registered as an S8 (Schedule 8) drug. These drugs are listed as both addictive & dangerous drugs, which is why only qualified Nurses and Doctors are able to administer the treatment.

The drug is the same as Morphine (all forms), Methadone, Pethidene, and Ritalin just to name a few.

For me when I take a closer look at the effects these lip injections are having on many women on an emotional level, I want to tell them to stop and take a closer look. And although I believe that there is room for all different procedures I do believe that many women don't have the full story and consider this form of treatment to be harmless.

The central nervous system is the key to helping our bodies carry messages throughout it. And when you block this you are more likely to feel depressed and less sure of who you are. The more often you have lip injections the more likelihood you will want more because you have that feeling of not enough, or not feeling good enough.

This is the separation between physical and our emotions. It is my goal that through reading this book you take a closer look and see if it really is working for you on an emotional level.

A few years ago I worked as an Assistant in Nursing. I had made up my mind I was going to become a nurse so I could offer injectables to my clients. I had it all worked out, I'd been accepted into university to do my degree, I had the perfect career lined up at a well renowned surgery and clinic, I was set.

But something happened as I began to delve a little deeper into the whole injections phenomenon and I decided to take a closer look. When I found out that it was classed as an S8 drug and was from the stomach of rotting cows and the same toxic substance that caused food poisoning, I had to stop and ask myself why this wasn't sitting well with me.

Given my back ground and understanding of the CNS I couldn't see how this could be a good thing for women's bodies. It didn't seem right to me and in that moment I realised I couldn't inject poison into people's lips or faces.

It's important to always do your homework when it comes to things being put in your body. It's up to you to do it, and I really hope that this book has helped you in some way to see and learn new things about your lips and you.

Remember natural doesn't always mean things are safe, but if you do choose to undertake these procedures my suggestion is to send it love. Remember when we spoke about the power of words and what they can do to you!

The Central
nervous system
effects
your entire body,
especially
your lips

Chapter 5

Lip procedure ingredients

With so many treatments available it's crucial to know what you are putting in your lips and where the ingredients are derived from and why they are used.

It's essential to find out where exactly any filler comes from and which questions you should ask. Most fillers are derived from animal body parts, such as roosters' combs, bovine and calf tissue, fish scales and many other ingredients.

It's your physician's job to help you understand more about 'exactly' what you are putting in to your lips. For example, even though Hyaluronic Acid is a naturally occurring compound found in the joints and skin tissue of humans, if you opt for lip injection procedures you should know that this form of Hyaluronic Acid will more than likely come from a laboratory or non-human animal tissue.

Always ask questions and listen to the answer. For example, if you ask your doctor what product they will be using in the procedure and the answer is "We use a highly effective natural occurring Hyaluronic Acid from [and states the company name]", you haven't actually been told where it comes from.

Get your doctor to be honest with you, and ask where exactly this particular HA has come from, as it could come from something that you are not comfortable having in your body.

Here's some tips and questions to ask

- How long have you been doing this?
- What is the exact ingredient used in your product?
- What allergic reactions should I be aware of?
- Where do you buy your supplies?
- Ask to see the full list of ingredients.
- Do your research first.
- Check the credentials.
- Is it tested on animals?

Be mindful of exactly what it says on the label and dig a little deeper if you have to, as not all labels will have the entire list of ingredients on them. Look at the back of the container and don't rely on the front to tell you what it contains.

Fortunately, if you choose to follow a more sustainable and natural approach to your luscious lip care desires you will find that there is a range of products and ingredients that restore your own collagen. The key is to opt for ingredients that are protein based because these are the basic fundamentals that restore the hydration and collagen in your lips.

Top seven protein based ingredients your lips will love

1. Organic bee pollen (40%)
2. Organic Goji Berries (approx. 20%)
3. Spirulina (57%)
4. Hemp Seed (33%)
5. Soya Beans (40%)
6. Chia Seeds (20%)
7. Almond oil (21%)

Chapter 6

Lip-spa

Have you tried doing lip-spa exercises before? These fun exercises can help you reduce stress, minimise fine lines, increase blood flow and gives your lip area an all over glow. You can do them virtually anywhere, even when you're at work, driving or sitting on your couch.

These fun lip-excises are a great way to improve your jaw line, jowl lines and lip lines. They may even help minimise your fine lines.

No 1: Lip tapping and mantras

I know this will seem slightly weird but it really does help improve your overall wellbeing. By tapping the top of your lip area in the centre and then moving around your lip area in a clock wise motions with an *'I am'* **mantra** will make a huge difference. Always start at the centre top lip, tap for seven times on each spot from the top centre to the corner to bottom centre to corner again, repeat as often as you like and extend your time to around five minutes.

No 2: Bubbly cheeks

Take a mouthful of air so it expands your cheeks (like you would if your holding your breath). Move the air from top to bottom and side to side. Do this for around ten times with an increase to thirty times. This helps to reduce stress that is commonly found in your jaws. By doing this exercise daily you are less likely to clench your jaw at night. Which may reduce the amount of fine lines around your lip area.

No 3: Lip stretching

Open your mouth as wide as you can by stretching your lip area hold for around ten to thirty seconds each time. You will find that you naturally yawn, which helps to eliminate stress.

No 4: Pucker up butter cup

Suck the sides of lips into your cheek area and move the lips up and down. Repeat for around one minute. This helps to activate unused muscles in your lip area. And it's a fun thing to do.

No 5: Tongue twister

Run your tongue around the inside of your closed mouth on the upper and lower lip lines. Do this for around one minute. Do it very slowly and change direction every five laps.

*For best results
try doing any or all
of these lip-exercises
for up to
20 minutes a day*

Section Six ~ One Kiss More

Chapter 1

The power of one

When writing this book people asked what the title was, and to be honest I had quite a few ideas that I played with, and although they had a great ring to them, there was something missing.

One night during a dream I woke with this incredible feeling of oneness and an understanding of the exact purpose for this special life I have. It's the kind of dream that you wake from, feeling both bemused and empowered at the same time. I knew then exactly what my book would be called; it had to have a greater meaning, like naming a child.

I really had no idea why I was going to call this little book about lips *One Million Kisses* and yet I knew in my heart, I had to.

A friend asked me why that name - what's the big picture - so I explained about the power of one, what it means in numerology and on an emotional, spiritual and physical meaning. She said, 'I think your readers might like to know that.'

Allow me to explain a little further; one is a primal number and it represents the beginning of new things. It demonstrates courage and stands alone. This is depicted in the way it is written strong and stable. There is no mistaking the number one when you look at it unless it looks like the letter 'I'. Which to me is rather funny.

One represents a unique equation – one is only dividable by itself. *It's pretty powerful!*

When I think about the power of one, I think about this little saying, "If it's going to be, it's up to me". *I'm sure you've heard of this before?*

This doesn't mean you shouldn't ask for help when required: quite the contrary. It's important to recognise that everything we do is about ourselves. Whether we like to think about this or not, it's true.

Yes, we can run around helping and caring for others; we can praise and give love to others, yet often we don't have any left over for ourselves.

For me, one represents so much in life, for if you don't care for yourself how can you truly help others who may be less fortunate? It's not sustainable and you will eventually feel depleted and drained. You might then begin to feel jealous of what others have, and focus only on the things you want. This can quite often lead to the beginning of diseases in your life.

The purpose of this book is to bring you back into balance. I want to help others think differently about themselves: it's what I naturally do in almost any conversation I have.

I truly believe that when you know better you will do better. Growing and learning is all part of the journey, and when we think about things happening 'for' us and not 'to' us, this can be truly life changing. No matter what the situation.

I believe that one person can make a big difference.
I believe that one person can create a life of happiness even after hardship.
I believe that one person can be, do and have anything they truly desire - and that has nothing to do with money, privilege or the way they were raised.

Likewise
I believe that one person can keep themselves feeling stuck and feeling lost.
I believe that one person can stop the flow of love into their life.
I believe that one person can keep themselves playing the victim in their life.

And
I believe that one person can change their life in one second.
I believe that one person can change someone else's life in one second.
I believe that one person can change their entire environment in one second.

The power of one (you) is infinite and your entire belief in you is up to you and no one else. All you need to do is believe, accept and understand.
Never be anyone else's version of you.

Your unique essence doesn't call for you to be famous, have millions of fans across the globe, or create a life-changing invention. Life comes in many shapes and sizes, just like your lips, and you can create one that's perfect for you.

It simply means to be yourself and trust in what you know. The more you practise the feeling of oneness, the better you will get at it. Just be you (one).

Being confident about who you are as a person, with all the different quirky bits, makes you you, and I believe in you.

My goal is to help one million people change the way they think about their lips. I believe that's why I wrote this book!

Beauty is
an energy
that transcends
time & age
it's gracious,
kind and forthright
it creates the
best relationship

with your soul

Chapter 2

The little girl with the scar on her lip

I'd like to share a little story about a young girl who was turning two. She was a lively spirited and very busy toddler who just loved to play, especially with her big brother and sister.

One day the little girl ran into her brother's room and starting playing with his cars and toys, whilst he was out doing other things.

When he came into the room and saw her playing with his toys, he began to push her out the door. But the little toddler who wouldn't take 'no' for an answer continued to play with the toys.

Her brother, who was only four, rather liked his things and was having none of this sharing caper with his little sister.

One thing lead do another and the little girl decided to get up and leave the room, but at the last minute turned and attempted to run back into her brother's room.

Her brother saw her coming back into his space, and quickly got up and slammed the door, which collided with the little girl's face with a sickening thud.

One second was all it took.

The little girl wasn't quick enough to avoid the hit and ran straight into the door, splitting her lip open. She ran down to her mum who tried to stop the bleeding, but soon realised she had to get her daughter to a hospital.

It turned out that the little girl, whose birthday was in a few days, needed four stitches on her top lip. The doctor said she would more than likely have a scar over her top lip, but not to worry as she was a happy confident little girl and it would heal without any problems.

A LITTLE BOOK ABOUT LIPS

That little girl was me, just before my second birthday!

I've grown up with a scar over my lip and I've never really thought any differently, because that's who I am. It's one of my unique characteristics and I'm proud of it. It makes me, me. I've always recognised my lip scar as a gift and my lucky sign.

Funnily enough the area where my scar is represents the creativity and vision section of my lip print readings.

I share this with you because the girls in the beginning of the book remind me that thinking about things differently can be truly life changing. I know for sure whether you hold on to things or not, really does make a difference to how you feel about yourself.

Every one of us has a story or a belief that we hold onto: it can either make or break who we are as people. Which will you choose?

Perhaps it was destiny that I ran into my brother's door that day. Perhaps that led me to write my first book on lips, so I can help others feel differently about their own lips. Maybe, just maybe, that's why I ran back as a little toddler.

Perhaps I'm only realising this some 45 years later.

Kisses

Janine x

CPSIA information can be obtained
at www.ICGtesting.com
Printed in the USA
BVHW04s1612030418
512350BV00016B/377/P